The Complete Sneaker Reseller Guide

Pro Tips from the Sole Master

Sole Masterson

ISBN-13: 978-1533316677

ISBN-10: 1533316678

Table of Contents

Cooking 101

Markets are a self-created function of the *Wisdom of Crowds* (an excellent book, by the way). In a free market economy, the forces of supply and demand will always move price to its perfect level. There's simply no denying this.

Sure, lots of would-be consumers complain about sneaker resellers, saying ignorant things like *they are ruining the market*. Nothing could be further from the truth. The market created us, not the other way around.

We sell products for double retail because a whole bunch of people are eager to pay that price for these particular sold-out items. While they were working, we were sitting in front of a computer clicking buttons at the exact right time, sometimes using special software loaded with the exact right instructions. The consumers never stood a chance getting these things at retail. For the products we cop, retail is the new wholesale.

Heck, if they want to blame someone, they should blame the manufacturers and retailers – who know exactly what they are doing, and even hire *demand creation marketing* consultants at ridiculous rates to tell them having a line around the block in front of their store every Saturday morning is good publicity. Duh. I would have told them that for free.

I can't explain why certain brands and/or certain styles within certain brands have so much demand the public is willing to pay twice retail for them in the aftermarket. I can only acknowledge that this situation exists, and teach you how to capitalize on it. The hype-reseller business is something anyone with a small bankroll can learn and get in on, and in a short while have a legitimate operation which earns $40,000+ per year for 5-10 hours effort every week (once you get the routine down). Those are conservative numbers, by the way. Teenagers using their parents' and uncles' credit cards have been interviewed who made six figures in 2015 running a part-time business before and after school. If you have the determination, it is possible to do this for a comfortable living.

What exactly are we talking about here? Just this: Buying and selling shoes, clothes, and cosmetics. The basic premise of the American dream, baby. Admittedly, it's a unique application. We don't need a business license because we are paying retail for our inventory. Did I say inventory? That may not be accurate, either – as many of us sell the product, including collecting payment, in advance of receiving it. When it hits our doorstep we simply slap a different shipping label on it and send it off again, having already banked the profit.

There are two types of aftermarket resellers. First, you have the power sellers. These folks run a full-time eBay business, don't mind keeping inventory on hand, and they buy-sell-ship stuff every day. As such, they are perfectly content to flip low-margin products and even sometimes take a loss on items that sputter and die. Their volume makes up for it. Nothing wrong with this approach. For years I worked in the auto accessory wholesale business, where gross profit margins were typically around 30%. The "custom wheel and tire" space sustains itself on profit margins around 20% (but they sell higher-end products). Buying sneakers for $130 which have a resell value of $180 can be part of a viable model, especially if you are able to utilize low-fee sales outlets. Sell three or four items today at $40-50 profit per sale and you can sleep sweetly tonight, knowing you did your thing. Remember, this is a home business with very little overhead other than the inventory. Even shipping supplies are mostly free.

Then you have the part-timers. That's most of us. We focus on high-margin items. Stuff we can double our money on, or at least make a cool hundie without tying up more than $200. There are enough high-margin drops to keep us busy. A typical week during the height of the season (late winter through mid-fall) has us cooking on 2-3 scheduled drops plus chasing at least that many sudden restock alerts. Anyone who has set themselves up with the right tools – and is able to pay attention – can score multiple items on a weekly basis.

Occasionally, the score will be huge. Think **Yeezy 750's**. Cop a pair of these and you're looking at a $1,000+ payday for a $350 investment. A recent Ultra Boost x Solebox release retailed for $190 and fetched $750+ in the aftermarket. Reebok "Alien Stompers" went for $180 landed and are lighting up eBay for $1,000 a pair – and they were not a difficult cop. As a reseller, these kinds of drops will all be on your agenda.

More typically, though, you'll be looking to double your money or thereabouts on certain Adidas NMD's, certain Ultra Boosts, Air Jordan Retro OG's, certain Nike Air Max releases, certain Supreme items, and stuff like that there.

Some of the players in the sneaker reseller business employ what is known as a *ground game*. This might even mean camping or standing in lines, paying others to camp or stand in lines, entering raffles, and/or paying others to enter raffles. You can find people looking to do this for you at online communities on Twitter and Reddit. You'll see Craigslist ads offering to pay $100+ for anyone that can secure a winning Yeezy raffle ticket. Your time is better spent elsewhere, in my opinion. With the odds of winning a Yeezy raffle somewhere around 1 in 75, it's just not worth the effort even if you score a pair of 750's and sell them for $1,700 on Flight Club. But there's nothing wrong with heading to the mall on a weekday to see if you can grab a couple hot pairs Jordans that are supposed to be restocking in local stores that day. Those can often be resold for a quick $100+ profit per pair.

The term "cooking" refers to using technology, that is a **bot**, to buy shoes for you on popular online drops. We botters get everything set up at least half-hour ahead of time, and then a few minutes before the drop we start our bots and watch, waiting for the beloved "checkout success" message. Because we have four or more accounts all hammering the same release at multi-threading speeds, our odds are pretty good.

Botting is only part of our acquisition strategy, though. We score just as many pairs of profitable shoes manually using web browser tricks, by being fast on the trigger reacting to restock alerts. This requires an advance setup as well.

Time for my first confession: this guide is associated with an inexpensive membership site that includes a forum and chat. It has live feeds piped in containing drop alerts, bot results, aftermarket evaluation, and industry news. We help and encourage each other there, review the various bots, and keep up with proxy providers. I'll be occasionally making reference to our members area as we go along, but you won't actually need it in order to succeed because I'm not holding anything back. The following chapters will provide **full disclosure** on teaching you everything I know for making a lucrative side income as a reseller.

The basics of what you'll need in order to be successful are:

• **Proper Banking Setup** including an appropriate bankroll

• **Acquisition Software** properly configured

• **Live, Breaking Information** (drop alerts & links) from the right sources

• **Market Evaluation** – the ability to predict resale value

• **Wise Selling Practices** so you don't get burned

In the pages that follow, I'll give you the specifics of the above points. Upon finishing this guide you'll have all the book knowledge of an expert in this business, and will only need some experience in order to complete your training. We can help you with that, too. So let's get started...

Banking Setup

You need several different banking identities. This is because limited releases only allow one item per customer, and you won't make enough money for this to be a worthwhile pursuit settling for one cop every drop. The magic number of banking identities for a part-time reseller is **four**.

Why four? Because there are four *Footsites*. In case you don't know the lingo, Footsites are the brands that reside under the **Foot Locker** umbrella: Foot Locker, Eastbay, Champs Sports, and Footaction. They are all Foot Locker stores, and thus all Foot Locker sites. Take that in. Each of their online stores are essentially differently-branded portals to the same website, as far as our identity is concerned. That means you cannot buy a limited release item, like say a pair of Yeezys, from Foot Locker and Eastbay with the same banking identity (credit card number **and/or** same billing address). If you do, both orders will be cancelled because of violating the "one per customer" rule.

By the way, limited releases are the dinner bell in this business. Low supply on high-demand products commands greater resale value. The "one per customer" releases are exactly what you are after – only you want to score multiple times on the drop. In order to accomplish this, you must "become" several different people with different addresses and payment methods. This is probably the most significant fundamental concept that separates the pros from the wannabes in the shoe game.

Let's tackle addresses first. Do you have any family living in your city? What about close friends you know you can trust? These are going to be your first considerations. Explain your new business to them and ask if it's okay that you have a package shipped to their house once in a while.

Doesn't work for you? No big deal. There are other solutions; specifically, **mail forwarding services**.

Please note that P.O. Box addresses are undesirable because many shoe retailers won't ship to them. Some do, but having a P.O. Box for an address on one of your accounts restricts your copping capabilities. You don't want anything restricting your copping capabilities.

These days, you can probably find multiple mailing center businesses in any medium-sized city. Many of them offer mail forwarding as well – it will take you a couple extra days to receive your product that way, but if you live in a rural area this may be your only option. In my city, for example, three miles from my house there is a business called *The Mail Center*. They offer a rented "mailbox" service and advertise the fact that my address will not be a P.O. Box. It will look like this:

My Name
16787 Nike Blvd. #_____
Adidas Beach, CA 90210

They also offer mail forwarding service, which I don't need. I like the fact I can drop my USPS packages off there as well, killing two reseller birds with one stone. The monthly fee for this is $21, and there's always someone there to sign for my packages.

But that's only one address. Isn't the cost going to be too much, especially if you need to use two or three of these places? Not really. If you maintain four banking identities, you'll be randomly distributing your cops across all of them. Each one will probably be responsible for at least $700 in net profits in any given month, so even if each address costs you $30 (and they won't) you're good. Don't forget all such business expenses are tax-deductible.

Got your four different addresses lined up? Good. Now let's talk banking. The way this is done is with **prepaid credit cards**. You can buy them at just about any drug store, convenience store, or supermarket these days. You can also order them online. Most are reloadable. Most don't do credit checks. Most let you change your address when you register them online, and some even let you change the spelling of your name (a good idea if you do not have a common name).

You need to understand how these work. The store where you buy a prepaid credit card will usually swipe your ID upon purchase as an anti-terrorism precaution, or so they say. Go ahead and fully load it with $500 right there at the cash register. Most cards will be usable from that moment, but at that point it works like a gift card. The way vendors verify purchaser information on gift cards is by name and zip code only. This is **not** what you want, because it will be too easy to cross-reference your multiple purchases. Moreover, some sites do not accept gift cards for payment – and they don't work with some of the better bots, either. No Bueno.

The solution is to take them home and register them. This is done in about two minutes online. When so doing, you can change your address – without any hassle – on most cards. Some will even let you respell your name. The second you complete the online registration process, your prepaid credit card acts like a "real" credit card with the online vendors. They won't know any difference when they charge it. That means they verify the name and entire physical address with the bank upon purchase, not just the zip code. Since the entire process is automated, your order completes – as it came from a different bank and different address than any of their other orders. (Vendors don't typically cross-reference names, because many people have the same names.)

The prepaid-card bank will mail you a permanent card after you register it online (to the address you registered, so make sure your stupid son-in-law doesn't trash it). The card you got in the flimsy packet at the store is temporary – but still fully usable until you register the permanent one, which will replace it at that point. To clarify: Once you register the temporary card online, it behaves like a real credit card with vendors and you can use it before receiving/activating the permanent card you'll be getting in the mail. The permanent card, however, is reloadable and usable at ATMs. The temporary one is not. Once you register a card, you cannot do so again with that same card issuing company as you are normally allowed only one account with each "card." So make sure you either get the permanent reloadable card, or use the funds up on the temporary one after registering it and then trash it in search of another. Which brings up the fact that...

There is a **huge** difference in fees among prepaid credit cards! They make their fees in different ways. You **don't** want a high monthly maintenance fee! Also try to avoid unreasonable fees for making spends. Small charges for a loading transaction are fine – we're talking under $5 here, but obviously load each card to the limit (usually $500) whenever you load. Many stores have a $500 total daily limit on loading prepaid cards, so you may have to go to a couple different places to reload multiple cards. Cards can be reloaded online via bank or Paypal transfers, but it takes 3-5 business days and you could miss some primo restock alerts in the meantime – so that's no good. Go to the bank, get cash, go to the stores and reload. Keep all your receipts in a tax file.

We review different prepaid cards in our members area, and you can Google search the fees for any you are considering at your local stores right there from your smart phone before purchasing. Two that we like are *American Express Serve* and *NetSpend*. One that we hate is *AccountNow* (and we caution you to be weary of the fees on all GreenDot cards).

Using **your regular credit or debit card** (with your real home address) for one of your purchasing accounts can be problematic, because banks flag too many transactions for unusual activity these days. If you have a bank who is cool about this, you can probably break them into the new pattern slowly, buying one pair of shoes online here and there. Also, you might be able to prevent problems by calling your bank before a drop date and telling them you'll be buying shoes online this Saturday and don't want any problems. Personally, I prefer assigning one of my prepaid cards my real info in order to avoid this scenario.

International Parcel Forwarding

We've barely gotten into this guide and already I'm about to drop a valuable pro tip on you that very few sneakerheads are doing (or even know about). When a hot shoe drops on the wrong side of the pond, you can still buy it directly from Nike or Adidas and use a parcel forwarding service for a shipping address. For example, the online UK stores for Nike and Adidas will allow you to pay with a US billing address as long as the shipping address is in the UK. At the time of this writing, a US Paypal account works beautifully as a payment method for Adidas/UK. For Nike UK you'll have to use one of your prepaid cards.

The reason so few people are doing this is probably because they don't know how easy it is, and/or they don't realize you can buy from Nike & Adidas UK with a US billing address.

Listen: It is **so** easy. You can open an account at *Forward2Me* in under 30 seconds. The first time I did this I actually had my shoes carted at Nike and was on the checkout page before I registered my parcel forwarding account. In under a minute I was checked out.

Your shoes will ship to the parcel forwarder, who will contact you when the package arrives to arrange for final shipping. It ain't the cheapest shipping and can easily cost $40-60 USD, depending on where you live, so this is only a tactic to use for high-margin sneakers. It works especially well for **Air Jordans**, which are nowhere near as popular in Europe as they are in the US. Often, all the retailers who offer US shipping will sell out within seconds of their drops while you can casually stroll to Nike/UK and buy as many as you want for maybe $30 in higher realized shipping costs per pair than the UK retailers (thankfully, Nike shipping is free and Adidas is almost free). But you also need to consider the unfavorable currency conversion when doing this.

Here is a list of good international parcel forwarders:

Europe to US services

www.BorderLinx.com (UK)

www.Forward2Me.com (UK)

www.Shiptronite.com (Cz)

US to Europe services

www.Shipito.com

www.MyUS.com

All right, you now have four different banking identities, meaning four different prepaid cards loaded with $500 each, all registered with different addresses. The next thing is to have four different **email addresses**. You are going to associate each with a different card. This is not for the vendors, however. Email addresses do not get verified with banks by online vendors for purchases. This is for the online vendors. If you need three more email accounts go make them at gmail, Hotmail, AOL, or wherever. Then create a spreadsheet and personally associate each email address with one of your cards. You are going to always use that email with that card when adding new purchasing tasks in your bots.

Speaking of bots, it's time to get those set up.

Bots, Proxies, & Servers

The sneaker bot scene is a constantly changing landscape. As such, the material in this section runs the risk of becoming slightly outdated. That's why we have a live members area with a forum. At the time of this writing, you can count the good commercial bots on one hand – though you'll need all your fingers. They are:

BetterNikeBot AIO Bot (Nike.com bot sold separately)

AnotherNikeBot AIO Bot (No Adidas.com support, Nike.com & Supreme bots sold separately)

Easy Cop Bot (Supreme bot sold separately)

Nike Slayer (Supreme, Nike, Footsite bots all separate)

Heated Sneaks (Browser-based, Nike.com bot is add-to-cart only)

Super Cop Bot (for Supreme on mobile devices but can only cop one of each item, not for serious resellers)

Now, there are doubtlessly some good private bots in addition to these which are not publicly available. And there are many *Chrome extension scripts* which only fill out forms for you. If you really want to search the ends of the internet, post a job on a freelance board for a multi-threading auto-checkout sneaker bot and programmers may hit you with stuff they have already made which is not being sold on any website. I've gotten good bots in the past for activities outside the shoe game doing that.

But these are going to be your main players, probably for the foreseeable future, as they have large Twitter followings and much motivation to keep their software current. That's the good thing about Twitter being the main hub for resellers copping high-demand products. It keeps the software providers honest. One glitch on release day and everyone hears about it.

The first four bots on the above list are quality multi-threading stand-alone software products. They are top of the line, and you should pick one of these to own. Please note that while these providers have excellent reputations for keeping their software constantly upgraded, warm & fuzzy customer service communication just ain't their thang (Easy Cop Bot being a notable exception). They are especially silent when it comes to advice on how to best use their software successfully. There seems to be an unwritten rule in the sneaker community that no one teaches anyone to cook. That's why I'm writing this guide; I recognized an opportunity based on a lack of supply.

The **Heated Sneaks** bot deserves special mention because they break the mold when it comes to instructions, tutorials, and communication. The only problem is their bot is one tier lower in class and capability, with the possible exceptions of Supreme and Adidas. (I say *bot* in the singular, even though all their "bots" can be purchased separately, because for all practical purposes if you are going to get one of them you are better off just buying the Elite package and getting them all).

Most of the Heated Sneaks bots are super-charged **web browser extension scripts**. Super-charged because they are far superior to any other browser-extension "form filling" bots/scripts you will find. Many of the HS bots perform auto-checkout for you, at impressive speeds. As already mentioned, their Supreme bot is superb and a good argument can be made that it is the best one to use, as it always seems to work and the massive number of success tweets every Thursday are undeniable. In order to use this product effectively, you will need to learn the Chrome web browser tricks discussed in the next chapter so you can have different proxies loaded in different open browser windows. (Heated Sneaks lets you run 4 instances at the same time, which is perfect for our four banking identities!)

The Adidas bot is the only stand-alone multi-threading product sold by Heated Sneaks, what some would call the "only real bot." Because the ANB-AIO bot (Another Nike Bot) conspicuously lacks Adidas.com support, the Heated Sneaks bot pairs nicely with it.

There are several other reasons to own the Heated Sneaks bot, not the least of which is the fact they constantly react to the market making new bots, and you get them free when that happens as an Elite package member. Two recent examples are their **Kylie Cosmetics** and **Palace Skateboards** bots. They also have a **Shopify** bot with auto checkout, which comes in handy during one-off sudden restocks at minor stores not supported by the big bots, because a lot of them use Shopify for their online store. In conclusion, at $125 the Heated Sneaks bot is kind of a no-brainer tool to have in your arsenal. You are, of course, also going to need at least one of the premium bots as well.

But wait. Bots aren't the only tools you'll need for copping the goods.

Proxies

You need good, fast proxies to run the premium bots. They are also extremely useful for web browser tricks when copping manually. Why do you need them? Because you will very likely occasionally get your IP address at least temporarily banned at certain shoe sites – and especially at Supreme – when hammering them with one of the premium bots. When that happens, you can quickly swap the proxies out.

A proxy is simply another IP address, or to put it another way, a different outside internet connection. The proxy providers serving the sneaker bot community typically sell you a certain number of proxies every month for a fixed subscription price. The proxies get delivered via text file, or even via tweet or text in the body of an email. They look like this:

192.171.245.4:80:username:password
104.144.17.123:80:username:password
157.94.208.181:80:username:password
178.222.7.192:80:username:password
122.171.235.67:80:username:password

You simply copy and paste them into the bot in the proxy-loading window. The bot then checks them and makes sure they are working (or you may have to instruct it to do so). Next month you'll get a different list delivered, and you can trash these.

All proxies are not created equal! Some will work at the sneaker retailers, but won't work at Supreme. Others will only work at the Footsites. If you plan on reselling Supreme items, make sure you get proxies that have been tested there, i.e. are designated as "Supreme proxies" (or contact the proxy provider and ask them about Supreme proxies).

No affordable proxies from the major proxy sites will any longer work on Nike.com. This situation is not likely to change. Nike is a challenge to hit for more than one banking identity these days. If you are going to bot the regular (non-draw) releases you are going to need to either pay up for ridiculously expensive proxies or find a cowboy provider on Twitter that can give you a handful of cheap "Nike" proxies that "sometimes" work. Don't laugh – this is actually one of the more viable options.

Nike drops the most limited releases via a lottery system these days, which they refer to as a "draw." Your odds are slim. But 4 x slim is much better than 1 x slim, and you may as well enter, as some of these shoes have $500+ profit margins when you occasionally score a pair. Proxy solutions for your different banking identities are more available (and less crucial) for Nike draws. We'll discuss this in detail a few chapters from now.

We maintain a list of good proxy providers catering to the sneaker community in our forum, but two of the more popular ones are **SSLPrivateProxy** and **Mexela**. The standard "dedicated proxies" from major proxy sites like these are good for some tasks and will work at many sneaker retailers including the Footsites (but not Supreme and the tougher retailers like End Clothing). Still, it's good to buy a handful of these to keep at the ready every month.

You'll also want to buy a small number of proxies from different providers, including some from the cowboys on Twitter. These are the guys that operate purely by tweet promotion and do not have a website. The quality of their proxies varies widely, but anyone working the sneaker community for proxy orders certainly has something worth checking out – especially if you see their customers tweeting testimonials on drop days. At $3 (or less) per proxy the risk/reward is favorable to just buy a few and check them out. As already mentioned, some cowboys can provide proxies that will work on Nike at least occasionally. Cowboys are typically an excellent source of Supreme proxies, and may be fast becoming the only game in town for those. We maintain an active list of these providers in our members forum and review them there, but I'm not going to name any Twitter handles here because a lot of these guys come and go. You might have some luck finding a few by searching Twitter for the hashtag *proxies* and even fiverr.com for proxy providers.

You need good, fast, working proxies. This part isn't optional. Don't bother buying one of the premium bots if you don't plan on spending $30+ every month on proxies. Even if you try to operate manually, without a bot, you will still need proxies. When purchasing from the higher-profile website providers, make sure you always buy **dedicated** proxies that are yours alone to use. With the cowboys you just have to take what they're offering.

The next tool is a little more optional.

Servers

Renting a server increases your success rate because you have a clean, uncluttered environment with a reliable fast internet connection to run the bot from. Windows, Adobe, or an anti-virus program doesn't suddenly come on to update itself clogging up your connection and possibly interfering with the bot operation causing your PC to crash. Virtual private servers, known as a VPS, can be rented starting at about $39 per month with familiar Windows operating systems. Even the cheapest ones will be faster than your home PC. One extra Supreme shirt or two extra Kylie Lipkits per month will pay for it.

Most sneaker copping pros rent a server to use their bot on.

A secondary solution that is free would be to create a VM (that is a virtual machine) on your PC and run the bot from that, keeping all other software off of it and disabling windows updates. Both Oracle and VMware offer free VM's. You do need the ability to install windows on it, from a disk or ...wherever.

You connect to your VPS by using the *remote desktop connection* feature in windows. The server provider will give you the simple instructions. Once the initial connection is made, pin it to your start menu. You will then always be one click away from your server. It is ridiculously easy to use a rented VPS from your home PC. The only precaution here is to make sure you rent a Windows-based server, not Linux, if you are not a tech-head.

We maintain a list of good server providers in our forum, but two of the most popular in the sneaker community are **Sneaker Server** and **eBotServers**. Sneaker Server offers a small discount on BetterNikeBot-AIO Bot if you buy it at the same time as your server.

Setting Up for a Drop

All right, you have a good bot on a server or a VM, and some proxies loaded into it. How do you set it up for a drop? This is where knowing how to cook comes in. Because you have four different banking identities, you are most of the way there already. At this point it's a matter of using your brain in an organizational manner.

Because I am most familiar with BNB/AIO bot, some of the following may be specific to that software. But all the multi-threading bots operate similarly. It's the concept that's most important here.

Remember, the limited releases are what you want; the "one per customer" items – only you want four of them. You have to set your bot up so you are four different people (who may happen to have the same name) using your different banking identities: different cards with different addresses, phone numbers, and email addresses.

That's right, you need four different phone numbers. Don't sweat this too much, because vendors do not verify phone numbers with the bank when they charger your card, and they never call. This is more for the shipping company if they have trouble with the delivery. Worse comes to worse you can use fake numbers. But seriously – you can't come up with four numbers between your cell and land lines, work number, friends and family? If not, you can buy cheap numbers from Skype and even put voicemail on them.

You are going to love your banking identity spreadsheet, where you keep each prepaid card associated with a different address, email, and now phone number. You'll be referring to it often.

Your bot will have a place for you to enter your different credit cards, so your banking identities are kept in the software ready to use. You can name your credit card profiles something; I suggest naming them after your email address. This is because you must enter your email address manually when adding a task (setting up a purchasing account) in the bot, and then choose which card to use from a dropdown list. So it's easy to choose the one with the matching email.

The bot will let you choose to have a particular card charged only once during the session. This is a good way to organize your tasks. You can only buy one item from each identity, so use this option and group your tasks by credit card. You might have each card trying to buy four different sizes. As soon as one checks out successfully, all other tasks for that card stop because you have the "one charge per card" option selected.

Now for a more visual example. Let's say Yeezys are dropping on all four Footsites at a particular time (which is usually the way it goes down). You can set up your bot to work all four sites, assigning a different identity to each site, using a different proxy for each. Once you have your early links, probably from SoleLinks.com, it's time to set the bot up. In a single instance of the software open, your tasks would look something like this:

Foot Locker Tasks
        Size 8 - emailaccount1
        Size 9 - emailaccount1
        Size 12 - emailaccount1
        Size 13 emailaccount1

Eastbay Tasks
        Size 8 - emailaccount2
        Size 9 - emailaccount2
        Size 12 - emailaccount2
        Size 13 - emailaccount2

Champs Sports Tasks
>Size 8 - emailaccount3
>Size 9 - emailaccount3
>Size 12 - emailaccount3
>Size 13 - emailaccount3

Footaction Tasks
>Size 8 - emailaccount4
>Size 9 - emailaccount4
>Size 12 - emailaccount4
>Size 13 - emailaccount4

Get the idea? In a perfect world one of each group of tasks has a successful checkout and you score four pairs of Yeezys for a gigantic payday. Remember, each email account above is tied to a separate address, phone number, and prepaid credit card number, as soon as one prepaid card checks out the bot stops trying to check out any other carts using that card.

In the above example, the ideal setup would be assigning one of your proxies to each individual task, using 16 different proxies in total. This is because multi-threading bots make repeated fast page requests at the sites, which is what gets your IP address banned. If that were not the case, you could get away with four proxies here, one for each email account. But when you multiply the fast requests x 4 you risk getting the IP banned for too many requests. If the bot begins to return **403 error** messages you should stop the bot, swap the proxies out, and restart – although that risks being too late. So if you are only getting one or two 403 messages, you might want to just let the running processes continue, especially on a Yeezy drop. Yes, a 403 server error means your IP address was banned at one or more of the sites. If you don't have that many proxies at the moment, just spread the ones you have out the best you can (and maybe don't go for so many sizes).

For reasons just stated, I prefer to use four instances of the bot open for the above example task – which is allowed with BNB/AIO bot. For this setup I assign maybe 2-3 proxies in each instance of the bot running. If I get the dreaded 403 error in one of the bot windows I can stop and swap without stopping the other three processes running. Also, this method ensures that by some technical glitch the same IP address doesn't get used at multiple sites. Not every bot allows multiple instances running, though.

Let's look at a Supreme example now. It's a little different layout because the tasks are all at the same site.

Supreme Tasks

Box Hoodie S Black - emailaccount1
Anorak S Gold - emailaccount1
S Cap Blue - emailaccount1
Gonz Camo Jacket S - emailaccount1
Rebel T-shirt S - emailaccount1

Box Hoodie M Black - emailaccount2
Anorak M Gold - emailaccount2
S Cap Red - emailaccount2
Gonz Camo Jacket M - emailaccount2
Rebel T-shirt M - emailaccount2

Box Hoodie L Black - emailaccount3
Anorak L Gold - emailaccount3
S Cap Black - emailaccount3
Gonz Camo Jacket L - emailaccount3
Rebel T-shirt L - emailaccount3

Box Hoodie M Red - emailaccount4
Anorak M Navy - emailaccount4
S Cap Black - emailaccount4
Gonz Camo Jacket L - emailaccount4
Rebel T-shirt L - emailaccount4

Take a few minutes to understand the above organization, because this is the difference between knowing how to cook and simply owning the software. Again, each email account is a different identity with a different name, address, phone number, credit card, and assigned proxy – so for this setup only four total proxies are needed. I mixed up the product targets in a way that gives me a chance at getting easier-to-cop sizes and colors in case demand is super high on any size/color combo. But I also duplicated a few that I think will have the best resale value. At Supreme, each person is allowed to buy multiple items, but no more than one of any style. So make sure your cards are set to allow up to 5 check-outs with this set-up, and are not still set on 1 max checkout from the previous Footsite setup example. Here you want to try to buy multiple items on the same card, just not multiples of the same item. In the prior Footsite setup, you were only trying to buy one item per card because you were only allowed to buy one item per card. Get it?

In the Supreme setup, with all these tasks running on multiple threads the chances of copping 5-6 items is good. You can do this every Thursday at Supreme, hopefully for a $300+ payday each time (and occasionally a huge score on a super-hot item), as long as the bot is working. In my BNB/AIO bot I would definitely break these task lists into four different instances of the bot, ready to *stop and swap* the proxy in any instance where I get a 403 message.

Now is a good time for me to mention that the smart folks keep running their bot for several after a Supreme drop, because of "restocks" (failed verified transactions and cancelled orders due to multiple purchase attempts of the same style). You can get an extra item on a lot of drops doing this, even if you have to reset to go after something you missed.

A lot of times when hot new shoes drop, they will hit a small number of retailers on both sides of the pond. This is what you want, actually – limited supply. It's nice to have a bot that has a long list of supported sites. You can run it on a couple European sites that have U.S. shipping one day, for example SneakersnStuff & Dover Street, and then the next day hit one or two drops at USA sites like City Gear or Nice Kicks.

It's also nice to have bots that can do both Nike.com and Adidas.com in your arsenal, although the value of Nike bots is becoming ever-more-questionable (more on that in a bit). Keep these things in mind when figuring out which software packages to purchase.

Web Browser Tricks

Bots will be the fun tool in your arsenal, but you usually won't have time to set them up for sudden restock alerts – many of which aren't botable anyway. Some scheduled drops aren't botable, either. Fighting it out manually with a web browser is a **huge** part of product acquisition for a reseller, even if you own every bot out there. This section will help you get an edge over most of your competition.

Country-Specific I.P. Addresses

For retailer drops, your chances are better using a proxy from the country the store is in. But where do you get one? Some of the traditional proxy providers are willing to custom-tailor your monthly order, if you ask them, to include a few international proxies. So if you are in the USA, for example, you might ask them to give you four or five UK proxies every month as part of your package.

If not, Googling *private international proxies* will keep you busy a while. There are providers for $10 per month than will give you a handful of dedicated UK or US proxies (or Germany, or wherever). Some proxy cowboys on Twitter offer European or UK-specific proxies. These are good to have when a hot sneaker hits a non-botable overseas retailer that offers cheap international shipping. And this occurs all the time!

VPN services like *HideMyAss* can also come in handy. At less than $10 per month, the service is a no-brainer. They typically have a lot of servers in different locations which work at the minor online shoe retailers, and even one or two that work at tougher sites like END Clothing. You can buy the service for one month, try it, and if they don't have servers in the country you need that work at the site you need try a different one next month. Tip: The deeper you dig in the Google results for "VPN provider," the more likely you are to find a provider with servers that are not yet banned at Nike, Supreme, or END Clothing.

Changing Web Browser Proxies

Chrome is going to be your best friend when it comes to using proxies in a browser, with or without the Heated Sneaks bot. Why? Because of a handy free extension called *SwicthyOmega*, and the fact that Chrome allows different **user windows** (what Chrome refers to as "persons") to be run at the same time, each **working independently** of one another. That means you can have different proxies loaded in different open browser windows. If you don't immediately recognize the value of that, go get a cup of coffee and start reading this manual over from the beginning.

Let's discuss what happens if you **don't** have multiple Chrome users added and the SwitchyOmega extension installed for each user. When you go to your browser options and adjust the connection setting to use a proxy (in any browser except Firefox), what you are actually changing is the computer LAN setting. It works, but it gives you only one IP address to use at a time. All additional browser windows open will now connect through that same proxy, because it's set at your computer internet connection level. And you better not forget to disable the proxy in your LAN settings before a botable drop date or your bot probably won't work!

Firefox is the exception. It comes with a proxy setting feature that overrides the system LAN connection – which means you can use Firefox and Chrome (or Internet Explorer) side by side with different proxies loaded, but that's still only two. Any additional Firefox windows open will also use the same proxy. If you change the proxy in any Firefox window it changes all open windows to the same proxy. What's more, the Firefox proxy feature is unreliable and leaks your underlying LAN IP rather easily.

SwitchyOmega is a free Chrome extension that does what the Firefox proxy feature does, only much more reliably. That is to say, it lets you assign an overriding proxy to use with Chrome. But wait, there's more. It lets you add multiple proxy "profiles" so you can change saved proxies in two clicks of mouse, and it also stores the username/password for your proxies so you never have to enter them yourself. To summarize: this extension totally freaking rocks.

To get it, open Chrome and go to *Settings*, then on the left-side menu go to *Extensions*.

Search for "proxy" and scroll down the results until you see *SwitchyOmega*. Install it. A little circle will appear on the right side of the top of your Chrome bar. Click on it, and go to *Options* to configure. What you want to do here is create a *new profile*. Name it something, and load your proxy & port -- **then** click on the little lock image to load your username and password. Save the changes and this proxy profile will become part of the drop-down list from the top of your browser. You probably should add two or three proxy profiles.

If you've never used proxies before, they are broken down like this:

192.171.245.4:8080:billybob:checkmate456

Proxy part = 192.171.245.4 (just that)
Port part = 8080 (just that, after the first **:**)
Username = billybob
Password = checkmate456

Now, at this point you have the same problem you do with Firefox. Even with multiple Chrome instances open (from the same "person"), any time you switch proxy profiles all open windows will switch to it. The solution is to create additional *Chrome Users*. This will allow you to have independently operating windows with their own proxy. You don't need to register additional Google accounts in order to accomplish this. Just click on the little profile picture at the top of your browser, then click on *Switch person*, then on *Add person*. Voila! You just opened a virgin, independent, self-aware window. Now you need to go to Chrome extensions again and add SwitcyOmega to this Chrome user window as well. Repeat the entire process twice more and you have four Chrome user windows (persons) all with different proxies to use for your four different banking identities.

The next step is to set Chrome's auto-fill feature to store your address and credit card info for each, at which point it's almost like having a browser-based bot. Please note you can name each Chrome user something other than *person 1*, *person 2*, etc. I like to name them in a way that identifies the email, prepaid card, and shipping address set for each (using abbreviations). For example, one of your Chrome persons could be named:

NickgmailNetspendMomshouse

The ramifications of this are interesting for a person who has established four different banking identities, and even more so if that person is also renting a server. This is the setup for reacting to sudden restock alerts and copping multiple items. It's also the correct setup for using most of the Heated Sneaks bots, especially for Supreme. The HS bots do a much quicker job of checking out than you can with Chrome's auto-fill feature.

Disable Javascript (for Lipkits)

Kylie Cosmetics runs a Javascript redirect script that will allow you to get cart-jacked when checking out and send you back to the order page. Consequently, it is highly recommended to disable Javascript in your browser before a Lipkit drop if you are copping manually. Here's how:

www.wikihow.com/Disable-JavaScript

You do need to **re-enable again** it before using your browser at shoe sites, including Nike draws!

Auto Form-Fill

This convenient trick will give you an edge with a speedier checkout than much of your layperson competition. You can setup both

Firefox and Chrome to fill out many of the check-out form fields for you. Chrome is especially helpful because it even lets you store credit card numbers! Firefox requires an add-on app; there are several available, and they all make about 40% mistakes (putting your address in the phone number field, etc., but still faster than doing it all by hand). So again, Chrome is highly recommended here.

For instructions, Google something like: *Chrome Auto Form-Fill Instructions*

Clear Browser History

In case this isn't obvious, get in the habit of clearing your browser history often – especially your server browsers when you are fooling around changing proxies in them. You don't want to go back to the same shoe retailer with a different proxy two minutes after your last visit without clearing your browser history! This usually occurs when testing proxies you just purchased, especially in the days leading up to a hot drop or raffle.

The web browser tricks discussed in this section will be a critical part of your strategy. Many people who get into this business soon give up on the bots in frustration and stick to copping restocks manually. With four Chrome user windows always open, loaded with different proxies and your four different banking identities, all you have to do is pay attention to the right Twitter accounts and you can manually score high-margin shoes every week. The botable drops can just be gravy with this approach.

Backdoor Links

Some people are handy with website code, and thus are able to get an edge using what has affectionately become known as backdoor links. We begin to cross the fuzzy line into the world of hacking here, so skip this section if that makes you uncomfortable.

A backdoor link is essentially a link that the site isn't making public yet during the time leading up to a drop. It may already be uploaded, though, so you might be able to discover it through guesswork and/or scouring through the code of a similar web page on the same site. Once you have a backdoor link, you will use it to get your pair of sneakers carted ahead of the crowd. When zero hour hits, all you have to do is check out while everyone else (who doesn't have the backdoor link) slugs it out trying to get their shoes in the cart.

As a crude example, let's say a small online retailer has a link for a shoe that looks like this:

Shoeseller.com/airjordanretro10daffyduck_size_9.5

...and they are dropping a highly-sought Air Jordan 7 in a couple hours. The link isn't live yet, but you use a little logic and type this into your web browser:

Shoeseller.com/airjordanretro7mrmagoo_size_9.5

Voila, the purchase page pops up allowing you to cart a pair of those cool Mr. Magoo Jordans right now. This is an oversimplified example; the actual product links will most likely be a lot longer.

Backdoor links are mostly used on retailers that use **Shopify** as their cart software. We have some tutorials on how this is done posted in our members area, but here is a link to a decent explanation (plus a video):

www.bit.ly/1Q1ouMD

Product Targeting

So how do you know which items to go after? As Han Solo would say, *well that's the real trick, isn't it*? The knowledge of which products are hyped enough to create a high-margin aftermarket is what will allow you to make a decent income at this. Up until now, we've only been discussing preparation and organization. Those things are absolutely essential, but any wookie can learn how to get a few prepaid cards, put different addresses on them, become familiar with software operation, buy some proxies, and learn how to charge a high-powered laser weapon. Choosing your targets wisely is what will make or break you in this business, especially if you are going the part-time, high-margin route. It's so important we'll be focusing on it the next four chapters.

I'll be blunt: It's going to take some practice in order to get good, particularly if you do not belong to a private community (like ours) and go at it alone. It's only right. Should a green-as-grass noob be able to give a pro a competitive run for his money? Don't bother answering. I know you want it to be so. And to a certain degree it can be, now that this guide exists. But trust me, the pros aren't worried about you – yet, anyway.

As a noob, you are going to miss some lucrative drops. You are going to fumble with the software, racing the clock to get it set because you waited until it was too close to the bell. In all probability, there's going to be a learning curve before you start copping multiple items on a release. It's all good. You don't want to rush in and buy mesh NMD's when the aftermarket is selling them at retail. Take your time getting comfortable in your target selections. Buying the wrong sneakers is an expensive lesson you don't need. Walk before you fly.

To that end, I'm going to advise that you stay away from $200+ retail prices on all but the most lucrative high-margin items. The reason is eBay+Paypal fees come to **13% off the top** of your resale price. To put that in perspective: if you buy something for $250 landed and sell it on eBay for $300, your seller fees essentially devoured all your expected profits. Don't make this beginner mistake. Heck, these fees aren't pretty even if you buy something for $90 and sell it for $140 – but at least in this case you still have a nice chunk of meat left on the bone. As you can see, your **profit %** on every sale you make is critical. A good rule of thumb is to insist on **35% gross profit** on each expected sale when considering products to target. The easy way to do this is to multiply the expected aftermarket price **by .65** to get your max expenditure, and that includes inbound shipping! That means if you expect to resell for $250 don't pay more than about $165 landed. This will, regrettably, keep you off a lot of popular restocks. But hey, you're doing this as a business, not a hobby. Right?

Another way to beat the resale fees is to focus on shoes that are good bets to have a stable holding value over time. This means limited releases which don't figure to have an increased supply over the next few months. The highest supply level will likely be right when you get your shipment. If you can hold these a while, and wait for the supply to thin out, selling for a good price will be much easier. But of course, time is money as well, so the *investor* approach isn't for everyone.

Let's talk about **Yeezys** now, and get them out of the way, because they are an absolute no-brainer. This is the shoe the entire sneakerhead world chases with reckless abandon. It's made by Adidas. So far only a handful of style numbers have been created in two or three colorways each. The supply is extremely limited and the margins are *ka-ching ka-ching ka-ching*. I'm confident you can get your share of them even as a noob, whatever your share deserves to be. Obviously, if you have 40 proxies instead of 10 and six banking identities instead of four, your statistical share is larger.

You will make money on any Yeezy, any color, any size. If you can cop a pair of size 18's at $100 above retail, do it without the slightest hesitation. Just make sure they're not fakes! Buying from Adidas or their consortium sores assures you will never get a fake. But you can actually make money **buying Yeezys at aftermarket prices**, as long as the shoes are real, immediately after a drop and holding them until December to sell. This is because the supply is much higher after a release, and much lower during winter. Throw the Christmas season demand in into the mix and you have yourself a winning investment. There are a whole lot of people holding Yeezys like they're gold or bitcoins.

Okay, what else? Ah, now it gets trickier. You have to monitor the hype, and constantly measure supply and demand. Don't worry, there are plenty of other targets. Nike and Adidas have caught on to this demand-creation marketing thing, and aren't about to kill the golden goose by dumping a glutton of supply on the market for high-demand style numbers. High-margin products worth copping are still dropped every week. Some weeks in spring it gets crazy trying to keep up with it all.

The following sneakers are **usually** good bets:

• Nike **Air Jordan 1 Retro** anything

• Nike Air Jordan with "**Retro OG**" in style name

• Certain Nike Air Jordan **collaborations**

• Certain Nike **Air Max 1** styles

• The Nike **Kobe Black Mamba** entire series

• Certain Adidas **NMD** Runners – especially *Prime Knit* styles

- Certain Adidas **Ultra Boost** styles, especially collaborations

There are quite a few others that come and go. You'll get the hang of this from watching the hype. The number one rule is: if you can buy it an hour from now, you don't want it. Only shoes that sell out within minutes upon release/restock are worth investing in. Always, always, always evaluate the current aftermarket demand before deciding to go for a drop. You don't want to get burned when Adidas drops waaaayyyyyy too many NMD mesh pairs on the market, for example. But you **do** want to chase that new Ultra Boost collaboration that is a limited release and has $500+ margins! One resale on a pair of those would equal the total profit of ten over-supplied mesh NMD's. That's nine fewer trips to the post office for the same net result to your bank account.

Sizes

The hottest sizes to target are the ones where supply least meets demand. Not surprisingly, then, the most common shoe sizes are not the best sizes to target on many drops, because more of those sizes are made. On the other side of the coin, you don't want to get stuck with a low-demand size, either. Work the borders between these lands.

This dynamic has created a reliable targeting size for aftermarket resellers. They are as follows (for U.S. sizes):

Men's best sizes: **8**, **8.5**, **9**
Men's secondary best sizes: **12**, **12.5**, **13**
Women's best size: 7
Women's secondary best sizes: **6.5**, **7.5**
Grade School (GS) best size: 7

The exception is a super-hot shoe like Yeezy, AJ1 Retro OG, or a limited Ultra Boost collaboration sporting ridiculous eBay margins, in which case you can chase any size. But you won't go wrong sticking to the above sizes as a general guide. Stray from it at your own risk, and only after you gain enough experience to be confident.

Clothing

The two main clothing lines we chase at the time of this writing are **Supreme** and **Palace** (Palace Skateboards). Both are deeply-entrenched in the skateboarding culture. That's why the hype exists. If it wasn't for skateboarding, no one would give a hoot and these clothing lines may not even stay in business.

Safe Supreme Items

Hoodies, shirts, & caps

Speculative Supreme Items

Jackets & jerseys

Safe Palace Items

Long Sleeve Shirts

Speculative Palace Items

Anything else – check eBay before the drop!

Safe Sizes (both brands)

Medium! ...and to a lesser degree, small.

Speculative Sizes

Large – check eBay before the drop!

Don't bother with XL sizes from these companies unless you correctly perceive an extra special degree of hype. Be cautious of large as well. When's the last time you saw a large or extra-large skateboarder? Yeah, there are fans and posers, but medium is the money size here. Small is usually worth chasing on the safer items as well.

Oh, and by "safe" I by no means promise you'll turn a decent profit on every Supreme hoodie. Some of these perform better after the drop than others. But you'll always be able to get your money back on them. Shirts are probably the best bets for always booking a profit – they are fastest to sell, and because they retail for less it's easier to find a still-enthusiastic aftermarket. The ones with traditional "Supreme" logos tend to do better than most of the collaborations.

That said, **Supreme jackets** have the highest return potential. It's worth gambling on a lot of these, and holding them until all the "relay sales" (*will ship when I get it*) subside from the eBay listings. A recent denim trucker jacket that retailed for $188 sold quickly for $375 on these relay listings. You'd be happy being one of those, wouldn't you? Not if you saw the prices a week later at over $1,000 and some auctions even hitting $2,000. It pays to know when to gamble on holding an item.

Cosmetics

A lot of us do Kylie Cosmetics Lip Kits because we can buy them for $33 landed and resell them quickly on eBay for $50-70 each depending on color and current supply/demand. These things drop 3-4 times per month and always sell out with 5-10 minutes. They are an easy cop and a great way to get your feet wet in this business, especially if you need to build up your eBay seller reputation.

At the time of this writing, the limit is supposed to be 3 per color per person. Not all colors are worth going after. Stay away from new colors until you see what the aftermarket does on them. Also, sometimes the website will simply not let you check-out 3 of the same color even with Javascript disabled in your browser. It is, therefore, safer to try to cop 2 of each color.

Highest Demand Lipkit Colors

Koko & **Posie** (especially Koko)

Using the Chrome tricks taught in the last chapter, and only going for 2 each of Koko/Posie, you can easily cop 16 good lip kits on just about any drop, and that's manually with your web browser. Using a bot is even easier. At $28 average profit per kit you're looking at $448 in gross profits waiting to be sold after each drop. Not bad. Of course, you'll have to print out 16 shipping labels and make quite a few trips to the post office, too – but this can be reduced by selling the lip kits in pairs, especially 1 Koko + 1 Posie for about $125 total (which is a hot combo).

Understanding the Retailers

Noobs get confused over the many different sneaker retailers the drops (and restocks) occur at. Part of the problem is the bot companies list all their supported sites in a big long list without telling you which country they are in. Even after you take the time to learn their countries, knowing which ones ship to your country – and what they charge for shipping – is critical to decision making on many drops.

To that end, we have compiled a spreadsheet of the primary botable sneaker retailers in regards to U.S. Shipping policies and have posted it here:

www.HypeSniper.com/SneakerRetailers.pdf

You can see which bots support which sites, where the non-U.S. retailers are located, whether they offer U.S. shipping, what it costs, and what the thresholds for free shipping are at. Under the Heated Sneaks column, **ATC** designates "add-to-cart" which means their bot doesn't automatically check-out for you at these sites (but it is impressive how many places it does).

When you are just starting out, you are likely to mistakenly think many of these supported sites are worthless and that all the action is at FinishLine, the four Footsites, and Nike or Adidas direct. It won't take you long to appreciate all the other sites supported by your bots, though – especially once you start looking for restock tweets. Even on major release drops, you'll often notice one of the more obscure botable retailers getting a piece of the action, and you'll be glad you have a bot for it. *Jimmy Jazz*, *SneakersnStuff*, and *END Clothing* in particular see a lot of action.

The four Footsites and END Clothing are notoriously tough on banning IP addresses. Make sure you have working proxies for these sites in advance of the drop date.

END Clothing and **Hanon Shop** don't allow guest check-out. You need to have registered accounts at these places, and it is well worth the effort to register them. U.S. residences should seek out a working UK proxy to access END for the drop, even if you used a USA IP address to create your account (which is fine). A UK proxy will connect you to their site faster, and it is my personal conspiracy theory that UK proxies are given preference on drops at this site.

In addition, END likes to drop their hotter releases via what they call a "draw" – but what is in reality just another way to organize the mad rush at drop time. You have to respond to an email alert to get the link, and then get in a "virtual line." Have your browsers open with working proxies logged into END before the drop time and keep checking your inbox like crazy. They give you 5 minutes to complete if your "turn in line" ever gets to the front, so using an auto-form fill script isn't necessary.

Now, besides the botable retailers, there is a **whole lot** of action that occurs at a bunch of smaller unsupported sites. Some of these offer international shipping; some do not. Some have reasonable international shipping rates; some do not. You'll usually get the drop alerts on these anywhere from a few hours in advance to a couple minutes after the release. The example I have in mind as I write this is *Foot Patrol*, a UK retailer with cheap international shipping that occasionally gets in on a desirable drop.

What you want to do for sites like this is use a proxy from the same country (again, a VPN like HideMyAss comes in handy for this) and your Chrome browser to auto-fill your credit card info. If using a VPN, disable the SwitchyOmega proxy, as you'll be going by your LAN system setting. That means working only one browser, though. If you desire multiple pairs, you can use HideMyAss on multiple devices. So, if you have a server, a spare laptop, and octopus arms, you can still take a whack at it from three accounts. Otherwise you can try with the VPN proxy from your home PC and use the server to do the Chrome user windows thing with whatever proxies you have. The more connections you make, the better chance of getting through, wherever those connections are from. But in-country IP's have the best chances at these smaller retailers.

Getting the Drop Alerts

One of the frustrations you will likely have when first starting out is missing some of the drops because you never got the alert. The sudden restocks are particularly notorious for occurring while you are grocery shopping. Unless you are glued to your data feed 24/7, this can't be helped. The best you can do is pay attention as much as you can, and grab the stuff you are around for.

Scheduled drops are, of course, much more convenient. These are the ones you know about days, even weeks in advance and can plan your life around. They are usually the major botable releases, and there is plenty of time to do your aftermarket research and get a feel for the hype. And the hype is always there on these, because it builds upon itself and becomes a self-fulfilling prophecy. So the big releases are almost always worth pursuing, unless you get a sense that too much supply is being dumped or there is a less-than-enthusiastic aftermarket feel.

As you may have surmised by now, **Twitter** is the main hub of activity and information in the sneaker game. It's where Nike, Adidas, the retailers, and the bot companies all supply a continuous stream of information on upcoming releases, restock announcements, and copping strategies. Perhaps more importantly, it's also where a handful of information aggregators operate, who never appear to sleep and are always able to provide timely drop alerts.

If you've never actively used Twitter before, don't worry. It's intuitively easy to get the hang of. After creating an account, you decide who to "follow," and then the tweets from everyone you follow show up on your home page in a continuous feed with the newest ones at the top. You usually need to scroll down a ways and see a couple dozen tweets in order to get caught up on everything if you are checking in several times per day – assuming, of course, you are not following too many active tweeters.

Using Twitter to get the drop alerts boils down to:

1. Following the right sources

2. Not following too many sources, as you want to weed out the noise (which you can also do by muting the tweets of any account you follow)

3. Checking in often enough to get timely drop alerts when they occur

As mentioned, there are a handful of invaluable sources for drop alerts. We have special aggregated lists fed into our members area, but two of the better ones are **Sole Links** and **Sneaker Shouts** (Twitter handles @solelinks & @sneakershouts).

Sole Links is an indispensable source for getting the actual links to the product pages before they go live in the days leading up to a scheduled drop. These are the links you will use in your bot or web browser. You can simply check their website for these, **solelinks.com**. They also post much in the way of news on upcoming releases, as well as a few sudden restocks here and there – although those are usually only tweeted. But they don't get every restock alert.

Sneaker Shouts somehow gets just about every sudden restock alert. They do a good job of posting updates on their website, too, but to be on your game you need to follow their tweets. So here is a pro tip for you: Download the Twitter app to your cell phone, and follow the instructions at the link below to set your cell phone to chime whenever Sneaker Shouts tweets:

www.cnet.com/how-to/how-to-set-up-tweet-notifications-in-latest-twitter-for-ios-android

Do, not, however, also set Sole Links to chime your phone – reason being they simply send too many tweets. You'll train yourself to become unresponsive if your phone is always chiming, like the boy who cried wolf – and then you'll miss some hot restocks you should have copped and kick yourself. You really want just one good reliable source for these cell phone alerts, and Sneaker Shouts is one of my top three choices for that.

You can do other things with Twitter. Probably a lot more than I even know about. One thing I do know about is the ability to create custom lists which follow only certain accounts. These come in handy. You can also create widgets for these lists, and display them in handy places like blogs and who knows where else. We do this in the Hype Sniper members area for accounts we see as being relevant to our cause.

Heated Sneaks is an especially good Twitter account to follow, as they pimp every release supported by any of their bots in an effort to sell more bots. You can get the scoop on every Palace and Lipkit drop from them, in addition to Supreme and major sneaker drops (which you should already know about). They do tweet a little too much, so their feed can get annoying at times, but there's good wheat in there among the tares. And most of their customers don't know anywhere near as much as you now do about how to best use their software.

The primary source for Supreme drop info is an Instagram account by the name of **j_preme**. Follow his account to get the early price lists each week. This guy does, however, sometimes go on hiatus for a couple weeks. During those times you'll just need to watch the Reddit Supreme community and/or pay attention to the Heated Sneaks tweets. The other Instagram account we follow in our members area is that of Palace Skateboards, as it's the only place they really post updates.

I honestly think you can make a couple grand per month doing nothing more than reading all Sneaker Shouts tweets throughout the day and checking the Sole Links website 2-3 times a day even if you fail to cop at many of the major releases. Now throw in the $1,500+ in easy money from Supreme + Kylie Lipkits and another grand from various miscellaneous shenanigans (aftermarket flipping, winning a couple drawings, & maybe chasing a couple restocks on the ground) and you have a decent little side business going. Get really good at this and you might double all that income. If that potential beats your current full-time job salary, and you enjoy this craziness, by all means consider working your way up into going pro.

Ideally, if you're doing this right, you keep a rented server on a remote desktop connection at the ready. One click and you are on your server, where, of course, you always have four Chrome "user" windows open which are set on four different proxies (via SwitchyOmega) and your four different banking identities loaded into the Auto-fill forms of each of those Chrome windows. But your various Heated

Sneaks bot extensions are also loaded into each of those user windows, each holding the same banking identity as the Chrome auto-fill form for that window. And, of course, your multi-threading bot(s) are a click away from opening as well, in case of a botable restock.

To clarify, a **restock** is simply a retailer getting a new allocation of a high-demand shoe. They happen both in-store and online. It's the online ones we are mainly concerned about at Hype Sniper. The day I wrote this, it became known from certain Twitter sources that Champs Sports was restocking Ultra Boosts in the much-desired chalk/cream color in their stores, which were sporting nice eBay margins of around $150. This news hit mid-day on a Tuesday, so competition would be light if I had a mind to drive to the mall and see if my store had any 8's, 9's, or 12's in men's sizes. Alas, it's difficult to motivate me to leave my PC. I'm an online guy – and I really needed to get this cookbook written. But if you are so inclined, you can physically make this kind of a cop on a regular basis. People do it all the time, and coming away from the store with 4 pairs of $150+ margin sneakers is not uncommon at all.

But I also know that because this in-store restock occurred, it's a damn good idea to keep an extra-close watch on my Twitter feeds looking for an online restock of this sneaker the rest of today, tomorrow, and the next day. These shoes are out there, shipping and hitting retailers, so they may very well hit one that decides to sell their stock online for a quick turnaround. And that alert will likely come in the form of a tweet from Sneaker Shouts that gives me less than 30-minutes notice, or maybe even after the fact.

Similarly, when certain high-demand sneakers **appear** to be dropping across the pond by Nike-only or Adidas-only, I say to myself *yeah right* and keep an eye on my Twitter feeds for a drop or two at minor retailers there who offer international shipping and might get thrown a bone (or, if the margins look high enough, I might buy them direct and use a parcel forwarder like Borderlinx).

Which illustrates another good point. When I first started at this, I used to fret when a drop got by me and figured I missed the boat. Nope. That's rare. Usually, there will be more – you just never know where. But that shoe has a good chance of popping up suddenly at other places, including some of the minor non-botable retailers mentioned in the last chapter. Stay on the alert.

Well, duh. You knew that by know. To do this business correctly you are always on the alert anyway, right? You have your Twitter account set and grab that cell phone 10-15 times a day to read the Sneaker Shouts tweets. When you're looking for restocks after missing out on a major drop, at least you already know the current aftermarket situation. That isn't the case with most of the sudden restock alerts. Those you usually need to do some quick research on before pulling the trigger. Let's talk about that now...

Market Evaluation

Knowing whether or not to pull the trigger on a sneaker drop, and deciding which Supreme/Palace/Lipkit items to target, is a learned skill that comes through trial and error. Even pros get burned sometimes by buying into high-supply drops for the simple reason that they neglected to do a few quick minutes of market research. Don't let that happen to you. Always check current aftermarket resale value before jumping on a drop.

The most obvious place to look is **eBay**. Be aware that you can get fooled there, though – especially the night before a major drop. You'll see some listings way too cheap, and others way too high. Maybe there will only be a few listings for this item, or maybe there will be pages and pages of what looks like way too many available. Sometimes you won't know what to think. Experience will teach you more than I can here, but my best tips are:

• Check all the **open listings first** to get a feel for the marketplace. Just search for the product by name, for example *NMD Chukka Black*. Take note of which sizes are listed higher than others. Click on a few of the cheaper listings to see if they are "pre-orders." Those are the guys using bots who are confident they will cop multiple pairs, and these listings are normally cheaper than what the market will command after the drop. Keep in mind the pre-order guys own all the bots, rent multiple servers, and buy $300-500 proxy packages every month.

• Then check the **sold listings**. This is the real pro trick. On the right side of your eBay search results you will see a list of filters. Down at the bottom, check the box that says Sold. The page will refresh and you will see what this item has actually sold for recently. Make sure there are some sales today, at prices which confirm the margins you assumed by the open listings. Take this information to heart. Remember, the actual market is what buyers are willing to pay, not what sellers are hoping to get. But also keep in mind that a **large number of sales** every day reveals strong demand which will likely push prices higher than they currently are! You want to notice **both** sold prices and the number of sales in a given day, and target situations with a comfortable balance of the two.

• Do another search for the product, but this time by the product **style number**. This is the manufacturer's stocking number and it will be included in many of the eBay listings. Make sure you get it from a listing that you can see is for the right sneaker. The reason for doing this is many sneakers look alike, and some unscrupulous sellers will list the product description for the sneaker you are searching for a less desirable shoe. Searching by product number cleans out the trash and also gives you a different market perspective on the listing results, which can occasionally be enlightening.

• Sometimes you can gauge the demand by correctly perceiving they hype around a product on Twitter. When the alert feeds, the bot companies, and a lot of individuals following them all start chattering about a certain drop, you know it will be high-demand. In these cases you can allow for an unusually high number of cheap preorder listings on eBay as long as there are also multiple same-day sold listings.

• On a close call lean towards passing. If the margins are a little thin, the cost is a little high, there are a zillion listings, and only three or four sales every day, pass.

• Conversely, be willing to gamble more on a shoe with very few listings, even if none have sold. The hype is missing, but the low supply works in your favor. Just make sure the retailers and manufacturer are all sold out of it. Understand you may have to sit with that shoe a while. Maybe get this one in your size, just in case – especially if you like it.

Flight Club

Another pro tip here. This is the top sneaker consignment store on the internet and they are a class act six ways from Sunday. Because they are so trusted, they can – and do – command the top prices on the highest-demand sneakers. Think of them as the sneaker provider to the stars.

But even Flight Club cannot sell over-supplied shoes higher than retail. In fact, one of the surest ways to know to stay off a drop is if Flight Club has that shoe listed at (or slightly above) retail. This is exactly what happened on the massive NMD drop that occurred while this guide was being written. Adidas made a **ton** of the mesh styles this time around. Last time, they were a nice $100-margin on a $120 shoe. This time Flight Club had them listed at retail in the days before the first drops hit. A whole lot of over-anxious noob resellers gobbled them up anyway. The pros stayed away. In all fairness, the hype did build upon itself enough to clear out all stocks and end up creating $50 gross margins in the aftermarket. If you are a full time power-seller, fine – but it was still much wiser to wait until the market settled before jumping in, as there were many subsequent easily-copped restocks, including simply buying them at the mall on weekdays.

As a general rule, you want to see Flight Club prices higher than eBay listings. That's a normally-structured aftermarket. A good example happened recently on an AJ17s restock. The eBay sold listings were $325-375 and Flight Club had them listed at $450+. This tells you all is copacetic, giving you the green light to chase those $190 retail sneaks to your heart's content.

Supreme Clothing

Supreme is a little different, because usually no one has the product "in hand" before the drops. That means you can only really check the pre-order sales on eBay – but you **can** see some sold listings there, which is helpful.

Every Supreme item sells out on every drop, but not every Supreme item is worth chasing. We covered the safe items in a previous chapter. I'll be the first to admit that often an item or two hits that falls outside those guidelines which is well worth the effort.

What it comes down to is measuring the presale hype. This is difficult to do on Twitter. Thankfully, a hyperactive online community of Supreme enthusiasts exists which we can monitor. They reside on **Reddit**. Here is the link:

https://www.reddit.com/r/supremeclothing/

I have gotten particularly good at predicting the highest-demand items on every drop by simply spending an hour reading the threads on Reddit about "this week's drop." These guys wear their heart on their sleeves and telegraph every pass. Many of your aftermarket customers are members of this community! I usually come away from it with a couple good targets that many resellers miss because they are only guessing, going by history, and maybe looking at eBay. Not only do I know the best items, but the hot colors, too (and of course I always know to go after small and medium sizes).

Palace Skateboards is more difficult to assess because the drops are infrequent and there is no centralized community (at least that I can find) of enthusiasts discussing what items they are pursuing in a fever of financial irresponsibility, like with Supreme. You can find a few sparse threads searching Reddit and some conversations on Twitter, along with a thread or two on the above Supreme forum that may help. If you happen to have a knack for fashion, that may come in handy as well. Me, I stick with the shirts here, especially long-sleeves, and prefer the simple logo styles. Palace drops occur at a retailer (sometimes two), not on their own website. You'll get the scoop on your Twitter feed, probably from Heated Sneaks, but past experience will be your best guide for product targeting. Me, I'm sticking with shirts that have a triangle on them.

For **Kylie Lipkits** all you have to do is check eBay – but trust me, you will never lose money with **Koko** and **Posie** (especially Koko). If they ever drop too much supply on the market, you might want to give them a breather rather than make a dozen trips to the post office for $20 profit each. When they come out with new colors, its best to see what happens in the aftermarket on the first few drops before getting involved.

Execution

Copping is a rush. It can be addicting. When you're on a roll you'll feel like king of sneakerdom, and will be tempted to start buying riskier, low-margin drops. Don't let that happen. Always keep your business wits about you and only pull the trigger on the right stuff.

Ironically, the same problem happens when you're in a rut. After taking an L on three drops in a row you'll want to cop something – anything – just to prove the universe hasn't turned against you. Don't do that, either. Remember, you're just a player in a gigantic supply/demand matrix. Your ability to make an income depends on your decision making abilities and how fast you are on the draw. But this is like a police training course. Don't shoot the old lady with the grocery bag when she pops up.

If you live in the US, you are going to discover that copping from UK retailers can often be difficult with or without a bot. They typically don't get anywhere near enough stock allocation to accommodate the avalanche of website requests at zero hour. Your chances aren't great with or without UK proxies, with or without a multi-threading bot. Don't lose a lot of sleep over these drops, and don't stress chasing them all. Do what you can and laugh the rest off.

You'll have **much** better luck copping European drops directly from Nike-uk and Adidas-uk using a parcel forwarder for shipping. A lot of U.S. high-demand sneakers are relatively slow to sell out from the manufacturers across the pond. But that extra $40-50 shipping cost will likely keep you off all but the highest-margin drops. So be it.

One of the reasons pros cop more than noobs is they don't have to do any market evaluation when a sudden restock hits their Twitter feed. They know the sneaker market, and can act quickly with confidence. Taking 60 seconds to check eBay and Flight Club will make you too late on a lot of these alerts. As a noob, though, you are still better off missing drops than buying unprofitable shoes.

Your **central command center** will most likely consist of a Twitter Feed in a separate web browser minimized to your taskbar, where a glance will tell you when there are new Tweets to check (it will show a number, just like a minimized email inbox). A remote desktop connection is pinned to your Windows Start menu which takes you to your rented VPS in one click.

On the server, four Chrome user windows are always open, perhaps minimized to the task bar, set on four different proxies but easily switched to different proxies with two clicks. Several text files reside on the server desktop with this month's proxies; each list is designated as *Supreme, Nike, Footsite, UK,* or maybe something like *Squid* (another provider). Your four Chrome windows have your auto-fill info stored for your four different banking identities, and are also loaded with your Heated Sneaks bot extensions (including their Shopify site bot).

Also on your server desktop is the shortcut to your multi-threading bot(s) ready to setup for the next targeted scheduled drop, which is probably not more than a few days away.

But that's not the reason you just clicked over to your server today. You just got a restock alert from Twitter. Twenty minutes from now, a certain European retailer is selling the rest of their stock of a hot NMD Prime Knit you tried to bot, unsuccessfully, at Hanon, END, and Offspring in two different sessions in the last twelve hours. You even left the bot on for the last six hours hammering away at Hanon and END in case of an unannounced restock. But no luck. So, you stop the bot for now.

This retailer is in Germany. The price is higher than you like, but you know it includes the VAT, and they have cheap worldwide shipping. When you go to checkout to a US shipping address, the VAT should disappear making your total landed cost around $200 USD – and **lots** of eBay listings have sold today in the mid-3's.

Now to get an edge. You switch to your UK proxies, which are as close as you can get with your current batch, connect to the link (which has a convenient countdown clock) and then do something the suckers aren't bothering to do – you **create four accounts** at this site, one in each Chrome user window, using auto-fill to complete all the information for each account including your billing addresses and credit card numbers, and make sure you stay logged in.

The clock expires and the race is on. You click a size, add it to cart, and click checkout – then while waiting you do the same in two other windows before seeing you can complete the order in the first window. You click to complete, and then try to repeat in the next window.

When the smoke clears, you copped two pairs! What's more, you see people complaining in tweets to the alert source that they got cart-jacked while checking out. It may well have been you who cart-jacked them. You smile, remembering the days when you were slow and dumb.

Manual Copping Tips

Don't give up just because the site says sold out. In a minute or two, all the failed transactions will be restocked. Keep refreshing the page, choosing a size if available, and trying to add to cart.

Keep both your US addresses and your parcel forwarding addresses saved in Chrome's auto-fill settings, which allows you to add as many as you like. For organizational purposes, it's best to have each Chrome user set with one of your banking addresses. With parcel forwarders you might only use two, so spread them out evenly.

Don't neglect this part of the business! There will be weeks when you get nothing by bot, but score $1,000 in expected profits using your browsers. Get into the habit of watching for new tweets.

Botting Tips

Always check for a new version of your bot before using it on a drop! Quite often, the site will have tweaked something the bot developer needs to fix for, and they don't get it done until a couple hours before the drop.

Similarly, don't use the bot's "scheduler" feature on any drop you care about. There's just too much of a chance there will be a bot update you need, and you will only get some of your proxies needlessly banned without it. If you want to cop that drop, get up for it.

When you take an L on a major botable release, check all the bot's Twitter pages a couple hours afterwards and see if there are complaints and/or success stories posted on the "tweets and replies" feed. Maybe all the bots had problems, and this will tell you. Maybe it's time to purchase one of the other bots that seems to be working better lately. Understand that those bot companies may be deleting all negative tweets which mention them, though.

Create accounts (at sites that allow it) before a drop and use accounts to check out rather than guest check-out. There is evidence that this increases your chances. You don't need to store credit card info on retailer accounts that you use the bot at, as the bot will complete all that info anyway.

Supreme Tips

Supreme likes to mess with the multi-threading bots on Thursday mornings. It's a constant battle. The bot providers will bob and weave and then Supreme will throw an uppercut at them next week. It's normal for half the multi-threaders to not work on any given Supreme drop.

For that reason, you'll be more consistent at Supreme using the **Heated Sneaks** bot, especially in four different Chrome user windows. That's our recommendation. Set the check-out delay at about 7 seconds for the best chance of success.

Restocks, however, are another matter entirely. Supreme allows the multi-threaders through on those, for whatever reason. These occur throughout the day on the Supreme site, especially 30-90 minutes after zero hour, but also at other random times – including even the next day! It pays to keep hammering them as long as you have working proxies.

Heated Sneaks also has a restock feature, but's browser-based so slower. At the time of this writing, the best practice is to use HS on the drop and then hammer away for the next 2 days with a multi-threader hoping to catch a restock (but save some of your proxies back so you don't get them all banned, especially if you just purchased them).

Winning the Draw

Taking their cue from Nike, some retailers, such as END Clothing, now sell the hottest drops via a raffle system. You have no choice but to enter these, as often the shoes will be an easy $500+ profit when you win. To increase your chances, you need to get all of your different banking identities entered in the drawings. This section will provide tips on doing that.

Let's talk Nike first. Nike has gone completely nuts in an all-out war against resellers and has, as a result, banned an insane number of IP addresses from accessing their website. We're talking entire subnet blocks here, which means all the IP's of all servers from all established hosting companies are banned. Most traditional proxy server providers can no longer provide IP's that work at Nike unless you are willing to buy a minimum of 50 for $600 or so, and even those offers are becoming rarer as more subnet blocks continue to get banned. This is intentional on

Nike's part. It still leaves all the ISP IP addresses, which they figure are the actual consumers.

Enter the proxy cowboys. At the time of this writing, there are a number of these operating on Twitter who can still provide working Nike proxies in small quantities at a reasonable price. I've noticed two things about these proxies:

1. When you test them on a "what is my ip" website they often return a description that indicates they are ISP based, saying things like "Cox Cable" from Omaha

2. They are usually rotating – meaning when you close the proxy and then access it again (the same proxy) in a few minutes, it shows a different IP address, source name, and location

In my opinion, what I just described is the future of sneaker proxies. The traditional providers will need to get on board with this kind of product or exit the sneaker reseller market. Cowboys might be taking over the business. I recently bought what was supposed to be a package of "new rotating Nike proxies" from a well-known website provider and they were so slow they were nearly unusable. But the hot new cowboy on the Twitter scene gave me fast ones that work at Nike, Supreme, and END clothing at half the cost.

No, I'm not going to get derailed in another proxy discussion here. Quite the contrary – I'm about to make a confession: Nike currently allows 4-5 different accounts from the same IP address. They must, of course, be different "people" with different billing addresses. Many sites are not as tough on proxies as I have led you to believe. Heck, even Supreme, who has a notorious reputation for banning IP's, will, in practice, allow multiple items to be purchased from the same IP address as long as it is from a different payment method with a different billing & shipping address. Same goes for many shoe retailers.

This is insider knowledge. If you own the BNB/AIO bot, arguably the best overall bot on the market (when it works), their instructions will warn you about how tough Supreme is on using only one credit card per proxy. That warning leads many to believe they must use different proxies for every banking identity. The truth is this simply hasn't been the case.

Different banking identities have always worked from the same IP address, as many Heated Sneaks bot users will testify – as long as you are using different Chrome user accounts. The IP bannings (at all sites) have largely been the result of "too many requests," meaning being hit too hard by multi-threading bots.

So why, then, have I been preaching proxies so heavily? Because a war against bots has begun, and I don't relish the prospect of having to rewrite this guide. I am teaching you good **habits**. I strongly suspect that Nike, Adidas, Supreme, and many retailers will soon crack down on IP addresses buying multiples of the same item. Set yourself up my way now, and you will still be copping when much of your competition starts getting their orders canceled. END Clothing has already gone this route. You need multiple proxies to hit them multiple times – and good ones at that.

Am I still talking proxies? Sheesh. All right, back to the draw.

Nike Draws

The Nike draw system is an actual lottery. The drawing date & time is usually published days in advance. The draw is open for one hour. There is no mad rush. You have one hour to follow the link (hopefully from four different IP addresses) and get all four of your banking identities entered. Piece of cake. Several minutes after the top of the hour, your four different email accounts will all have the dreaded "your entry was not selected" message from Nike – usually. Once in a while, you'll win a pair. Consider it gravy. These are usually high-margin shoes, so entering the draws is a no-brainer, all-reward, no-risk decision.

Only **cell-phone verified** Nike accounts can win the draw. That means you must use a different cell-phone to get a verification code by text message for each of your Nike accounts. Use your friends' and family members' cell phones for this. If you don't have any friends or family, post a "Request" gig as a buyer on Fiverr.com and pay people $5 to get the verification code for you on their phone.

Set your Nike accounts up with billing/shipping addresses and payment information ahead of time. Entering the draws is quick – you just choose a size, enter your credit card CVV number (or enter Paypal authorization), and click a few confirmation buttons.

Finally: By entering the same shoe size for all four of your entries, you dramatically increase your odds of winning a pair in that size. This does not mathematically increase your overall odds in the drawings, though. But it's probably a good short-term tactic, since none of us will live long enough for our total results to equal our expectation.

END Clothing

The END draw system, by contrast, is not a lottery. It's a mad rush and as such isn't all that different from a regular release. For that reason, there's a good chance some bots will support it by the time you read this.

Register for END draws ahead of time, any time after they are announced, from your four different accounts with different payment methods and email addresses, hopefully from four different IP addresses. When the draw goes off, you'll be frantically refreshing all four of your email account inboxes and/or Outlook looking for the link. You are, of course, already logged into all four accounts from your different Chrome user windows and/or your home PC and server. When you get the first email, click that link to get in line, then quickly copy the link and paste it into your other browser windows (where it may very well already be too late) to get those accounts in line, too.

Then you wait and see if you ever get to the front of the line. If you do, you have 5 minutes to complete the payment information – at which point it will save in your END account for later use (but not until you buy something from them for the first time). Because you have 5 minutes, the payment part isn't stressful. It's only getting that damn email and clicking the link to get in line.

END draws are tough on the high-demand shoes like Yeezys, and the best advice we can offer is to use a UK proxy to access them for the draw (regardless of what IP you registered your account with). Use bots if you have them – but don't expect them to keep working very long, because END is one of those places that are actively fighting against bots.

SneakersnStuff Draws

Stockholm-based SneakersnStuff does draws, too. They are more like Nike draws but even easier to enter. You just register an account then enter your email address, usually a day or two in advance, and they'll let you know if you won by email and give you a chance to purchase at that point.

Bots for Draws

At the time of this writing, BNB/Nike bot claims to be able to bypass the Nike draw system, meaning it can enter you as many times as you want with the same account and payment method, with or without proxies, and without needing cell-phone verified accounts. One person I follow entered a highly-lucrative draw 30 times with it, and actually won twice. Problem is he used the same Paypal account for every entry. He claims his Paypal account was charged twice, so he *should* be getting both shipments. Whether that actually happens or not is questionable. If Nike discovers it (which would be pretty easy) they will cancel and refund both orders.

These kinds of technology-tricks typically have a short life, so are not something you can reliably build a long-term business model on. Sure, you can keep up with all the latest tricks for gaming the system, but if you're not careful you'll spend more on software than you make back from using it because of the short life of the software.

Conclusion

Drawings are meant to be a lottery. Your only real advantage is having multiple banking identities allowing you to enter multiple times. You'll win your share in the long run, but your share isn't going to be very big. They are still worth entering, though, because it takes almost nothing in time and effort. Maybe you'll get an extra 1-2 pairs of sneakers a month this way. They'll usually be high-margin items when you score, so drawings could easily contribute $500+ to your bottom line.

Reselling Tips

All right, you copped the goods. Now it's time to sell them. This is the easy part, right? To someone with experience and/or a little marketing savvy, perhaps. To a green-as-grass noob, maybe not so much. Expect to Larry-Curly-and-Moe it up as a beginner on this side of the business just as much as you did on the purchasing side. These unavoidable lessons **will** pay off, however.

This is primarily an eBay business. There are other distribution channels, but they tend to be hazardous compared to eBay, with the exception of certain online consignment stores like Flight Club. eBay provides more built-in protection from scammers, not the least of which is a reputation system based on feedback from people you've done business with.

Which brings up the first important point: if you've never sold anything on eBay before, you won't have any seller reputation. That means buyers will be more wary of your listings than your active competitors who have established strong reputations. You'll need to be more creative with your listings, especially in your assurance that the product is genuine and has never been worn. Address these issues in your description, include photos of the actual product new in the box along with the invoice, and mention that a copy of the invoice from the retailer/manufacturer ships with the item.

Unfortunately, being a new seller also means you will be more of a target for scammers. It is therefore recommended to also include the following points in your listing description:

• No Returns
• Shipping to Paypal Address Only
• Signature Delivery Only (if item is $250+)
• No Buyers with Zero Feedback
• Signature Delivery Required for Buyers with few Feedbacks

The last two points can be a little tricky, so let me help you navigate them. First of all, **never** sell to a buyer with bad reputation (something under 90% positive feedback). Cancel the order and relist.

You also want to avoid zero-feedback buyers, and that probably includes any number less than five. Most of the scammers come dressed this way. Posting the above points in your listing should ward them off, but if you're not careful in your wording you could also turn away good customers. So it's a balancing act – your listing description needs to sell the sizzle, but it also needs to scare the bad guys away.

What do you do when a buyer without much feedback hits you? Require a signature delivery, just like you stated in the listing – even if it's for an $80 hat. (The one exception to this rule might be selling lip kits to female names, as that's a fairly safe transaction.) It will cost you more to ship, but it only takes one scammer claiming non-receipt to set you back 2-3 resales.

This webpage provides excellent tips for avoiding scammers:

www.NewLifeAuctions.com/ebay_scams.html

Follow those tips and you'll be protected from the non-receipt scam. But there are still two types of scams they can get you with: **unauthorized charge**, in which case Paypal will work with you to get the item back, and

fake merchandise claimed, in which case you are probably screwed, as the scammer will simply show Paypal pictures of fakes and claim they came from you (in these cases Paypal tells the scammer to destroy the fake merchandise and refunds them your money). Selling to buyers with good reputation is your best defense against this stuff.

Listing Tips

The most popular listing method is *Buy it Now* with *Best Offer* enabled. Sometimes I like to include a sign that says "Make Offer" in my primary photo (I actually add the sign on my PC via *Paint*). Then I put a bold note in the listing that says "Looking for Offers from Good-Reputation Buyers." When you do this, no one will buy it at the listed price. You'll be able to pick, choose, and negotiate with buyers that you see have established positive feedback. The drawback to this approach is many people do not like to haggle, and just want to buy a product at a decent listed price, so you lose that segment of the market – which is significant.

As a new seller, you are simply going to have to resell your items cheaper. This is part of building your business up. One bit of good news is that if you have used eBay to purchase products in the past you will have an established buyer reputation, which shows next to your listing, and many potential customers won't know the difference. But seasoned eBay buyers will. You'll notice the power-sellers commanding higher prices than you can. One day you'll get there!

There are, of course, other listing types besides *Buy it Now*. You can also sell by auction or by a combination of auction + Buy it Now. Feel free to experiment based on what you see your competitors doing, but understand three points: First, attaching Buy it Now to an auction pretty much assures no one will "buy it now" unless you get enough bids to push the price close to it. Second, auctions are risky – if there is a lot of supply at the moment, you'll end up selling the item cheaper than desired most of the time, and setting a high reserve in such cases usually renders the auction an exercise in futility. Auctions with no reserve attract more watchers. Finally, if you have multiples of the same item to sell you can only do it via the same listing through a straight Buy it Now listing (with or without Best Offer enabled). But you can easily send one of those items to an auction using eBay's *Send to Auction* button on your listings page, and eBay will reduce the quantity number of your Buy it Now listing by one.

The day your product hits your porch, you will probably want to get it up on eBay. The first step is to take another look at the market landscape for that item. Don't be surprised if it's changed, especially if you copped this pair of sneaks with a bot on a major drop. All your competitors are also getting their pairs delivered right about now, so the supply for this style number has probably jumped significantly. You need to consider this phenomenon when deciding whether or not to chase the drop in the first place. Sometimes it's better to hold a particular item until the supply dwindles. (This is also why I like manually copping limited, sudden restocks better than botting the larger scheduled releases.)

The most important thing to look at now are the Sold listings. Hopefully, there are at least a handful of sales happening every day. If not, you have just become a sneaker *investor* as opposed to a reseller. See which type of listings are selling the most: Buy it Now, best offers accepted, or auctions. List yours the way that is currently working – or, to be creative, if all the active listings are Buy it Now consider doing an auction so you stand out from the crowd. You can choose one of the sold listings you like to create yours from by clicking the "sell similar" button and then tweaking it with your details – which is by far the quickest and easiest way to create a new eBay listing.

The other important factor to take note of is how many pairs in **your size** are currently listed. If there's a bunch, you might need to hold that pair a while, or try selling through another avenue. I personally find that half-sizes are often in lower supply after a big drop (making US size 8.5 a smart size to go for).

Here's something many beginners have a hard time grasping: when listing your item for sale, your cost is no longer a factor, at all. It is **100% irrelevant** at this point. You are now the sales and marketing guy. If the purchasing guy screwed up, go see him later and give him an earful. List your product in a way, and at a price, that gives it the best chance of selling quickly but at a decent price near the middle of the range. Here is where Han Solo would again step in and say *that's the real trick, isn't it*? You'll get the hang of it. But don't feel like you need to be one of the cheapest listings, especially if you have some eBay reputation already. Being a bottom-feeder attracts the wrong kind of customers, anyway.

Once your listing is live, you will begin to get strange-sounding messages from people who want to do the transaction outside of eBay with you, by direct Paypal invoice. The premise is that this avoids the eBay fees, so should give you an excuse to lower your price. It's not allowed, and eBay doesn't like it. Also, this is the way scammers prefer to operate. That should be all I need to tell you about this practice. I tend to just ignore those messages.

eBay fees are not to be taken lightly, however. At 10% off the top of your gross sale, they are a formidable adversary to your bottom line. Add the 3% Paypal fees and you'll be breaking even on some resales that look profitable on the surface. Taking this grim reality into consideration is purchasing guy's job, though, not yours. You may need to have a sit-down with him and get him to stop chasing low-margin items. Your job, Mr. sales and marketing guy, is to not compound the inherit challenges of this business by getting scammed. Just one such incident will not only set you back further than you can tolerate this month, but it will rattle you and throw you off your game. You can't have that. Do things right.

eBay does a decent job of marketing your listing on the back end to those who view it – which means the most important thing for your listing is to get some eyeballs on it. This you do primarily by experimenting with different titles to get people to click to read it. Once that happens, eBay will email them every time you lower the price or when the time starts running out. So a wise marketing tactic, once you have a decent number of views, is to keep lowering the price by small amounts. It may also be a good idea to try a different HTML layout in your description each time, and maybe some different wording, too, since the last description didn't result in any of these people pulling the trigger.

Photos

Your listing photos must be a minimum of 500 pixels on the longest side or eBay will reject them. This is an issue when crunching photo sizes to email yourself from your cell phone or using product images you save from Google searches. You can resize your picture using Paint (usually by simply right-clicking the image and selecting Edit) or with a free online image resizer. My favorite one is at:

www.PicResize.com

Pre-orders

As already mentioned, some listings are for items the seller has not yet received, and some are even for items the seller has not yet acquired! Those offering pre-orders typically really know what they are doing. So, should you do it?

Regarding pre-orders: **no**. You'll get your reputation dinged when you fail to cop. This is for pros only.

When it comes to items you've copped but have not yet received, however, this is a perfectly acceptable way to operate and a good way to replenish your working capital. In your listing description, simply explain that the item has been shipped to you and that you will **turn around and ship it** to your customer the same day you get it. Some people like buying these types of listings because it makes them feel they are beating the crowd. They are still caught up in the hype, which makes them a desirable customer. Make sure you get shipping confirmation with a tracking number before listing it.

When it comes to **Supreme**, it is usually recommended that you list and sell your items this way, via a "relay" sale, as soon as you have shipping confirmation from them. Sell while the hype is still hot! Next week another drop list will be released, whereupon a bunch of your potential customers will suddenly decide they can live without your items. The exception to this advice is with certain higher-cost jackets you decide to gamble on, in which case you will wait until the item is in hand – or perhaps even longer – before listing it. This can really pay off on occasion.

Dressing up Your Listing

You don't have to sell your products with a drab, boring, unprofessional-looking listing description. eBay allows HTML, so use it. No, you don't need to know anything about HTML! Simply use one of the many free online editors, or, better yet, one of the free templates available. Snazzy-looking listings tickle people's buying bones.

I like to include images in the description – maybe small cute icons around the title and a standard product image from the manufacturer. Images in your listing description must be first uploaded somewhere else, and you insert them in your listing using the URL of the image. If you are using one of your own photos, you can upload it to **PostImage.org** and even resize it there.

Here are some good free online HTML editors for creating eBay listing descriptions:

Free Online HTML Editor:

www.BestOnlineHtmlEditor.com

Premade eBay Listing Templates:

www.SellerCore.com/free-auction-templates.php

www.FreeBoutiqueTemplates.com

www.Share-Your-Design.com

www.FreeAuctionDesigns.com/template

Shipping Tips

• Listings with **Free Shipping** stand out. This is an attractive feature, and often all a teetering customer needs to be pushed into hitting your *Buy it Now* button. When starting out, this is the way to go. Shoot for the quick turnaround and work on raising your margins after your reputation is built. Check the "offer free shipping box" when you create your listing, and then highlight this aspect of your offer again in your description to remind them.

• Everyone pretty much uses USPS, so it is a standard, expected shipping method by eBay buyers. Use Priority Mail so there is a tracking number.

• From **My eBay** you can order a variety of Priority Mail boxes, all **free**, and have them delivered to your home, free – so you have them on hand.

• For lip kits you probably need to visit your post office (or just go to an office supply store like Staples) and buy some bubble-wrap insulated envelopes, although this risks crushing the lip kit box and upsetting your customer. Small flat rate boxes can be used to avoid that, and these are free.

• Upon sale you can do **everything** from My eBay – pay for shipping (from your Paypal account), then print the shipping label and even have your mail carrier pick the package up at your house – or, if you drop it at the Post Office, there's no waiting in line. eBay does the rest for the customer (tells them it's shipped and tracks it for them). You don't need expensive labels! Print the label on paper and use clear shipping tape to attach it. You're done. If selling by direct Paypal invoice, you can purchase shipping labels in like manner from Paypal.

• Pick up a cheap **shipping scale** for your home office. You may not need it, as eBay does a good job of estimating your product weight for you, but you'll be more confident when purchasing shipping labels if you weigh the package yourself. The other way is to use your bathroom scale by repeatedly weighing yourself with and without the package in your arms – which means you have to look at your weight on the scale all the time. No Bueno.

• **Insure** sneakers & clothing items directly from eBay. It's cheaper than what USPS charges, and eBay is much easier to file a claim with. You don't need to insure lip kits, because when you print the label from eBay you get $100 insurance free. For every $100 in value above that it's only $1.65 to buy the insurance, a no-brainer and absolute necessity in securing protection from scammers and package thieves. So for Supreme hoodies, for example, spend the extra $3.30. If your buyer's reputation isn't as solid as you prefer, further spend the extra money to get a signature delivery!

• By default, on items $750 or higher (think Yeezys) eBay has signature delivery required set. That's way too high. You are only protected by Paypal on sales **$250 or higher** if it was a signature delivery.

Other Selling Venues

Never meet a stranger to sell a pair of sneakers. People have been assaulted and robbed doing this. It's insane, but it's all part of the sneaker hype. This is essentially the same crime as mugging you for your wallet. People who would never do that will jack you for a pair of Jordans, though.

Some people do sell Kylie Lipkits through Craigslist and that is probably okay. Have the customer meet you at a restaurant bar during happy hour. You were going to be there anyway, right? So it's convenient.

Amazon works like eBay's *Buy it Now* system but without the protection of buyer/seller reputation in place, and without the convenience of printing postage-paid printing labels at home. You'll have to handle postage and shipping yourself. The action on Amazon is slower, and mostly used by those with a larger inventory to offload.

Flight Club is a great place to sell high-margin shoes like Yeezys if you are willing to wait to get a good price. If you don't live near New York or Los Angeles you'll need to ship the shoes to them, but that cost (plus Flight Club's 20% commissions) will be more than offset by the higher price they'll get for your shoes. Highly recommended.

Stadium Goods is similar to Flight Club, but probably only a viable option if you live in New York.

Goat App is an interesting venue for reselling sneakers. You'll get higher prices than eBay for high-demand shoes here, and you sell/ship directly to the customer yourself. It takes a while to become an approved seller with them, though. You also have to ship your shoes to them for authentication – then they ship them back to you. So it's a bit of a hassle, but an interesting venue nonetheless and worth watching.

Twitter can be used to sell items as well. But this is a great place to get scammed. I would only do business with those who are running a business such as a bot seller or proxy cowboy and thus have a reputation to protect. Any time you put yourself in a position where you could get scammed, insure the package and require a signature delivery, even if you have to stand in line at the post office in order to do so.

Advanced Selling Strategies

Circumventing the 13% eBay+Paypal fees is highly desirable and can make the difference between having a side business and a hobby, especially if you like to go for those $50 margin restocks. You'll need to figure out a way to sell them yourself, whether via

Twitter, Craigslist, other social networks, online forums, a local flea market, or perhaps by cultivating your own mailing list of sneakerheads over time. (Just don't use eBay to solicit non-eBay sales. Besides being unethical, it can lead to your eBay account being suspended.) Direct Paypal invoicing is reasonably safe on lower-cost, not overly-hyped items as long as you only ship to confirmed Paypal addresses and require a signature delivery.

Selling on Twitter can be effective, assuming you have a good list of sneakerhead accounts to tweet at. We maintain a list of these accounts in our members area, but you can build one yourself rather easily. Just search Twitter for a popular sneaker that dropped recently and look for a photo of it in the tweet results; it will probably be an offer to sell and be addressed to several of these type accounts. Look at that person's other tweets. Make a note of these accounts they tweeted the offering to, go to those account pages and search all their "tweets and replies" looking for similar tweets and check out the accounts those tweets were copied to as well. Build up your own list this way. These sneakerhead Twitter accounts do typically have a reputation to protect, so the risk of getting scammed is lower. This tactic can be effective for pairs you are willing to sell at a low margin, especially if you can get retweets from accounts with a lot of followers (it may even be worth offering to pay for a retweet from certain people). Don't copy to more than three or four people on each tweet or the chances of getting a retweet dwindle. Your chances at getting retweets is also higher if you follow these accounts – but you should probably mute them.

Craiglist ads can sell a few pairs for you if you live in a large market. The advantages to doing a few cash transactions over the course of the year are attractive. Make the customer come to your house! Put something in the ad that will scare away robbers without sounding like a jerk – for example, you can humorously mention that you'll make sure your crazy gun enthusiast brother stays in his room while they are at your house. Tell them they must come alone or you won't open the door. I live in a gated community where license plates are logged upon entry, so I mention that as well.

For Americans, listing your sneakers on the **UK eBay site** can be a way to beat the eBay fees, and thus a good selling venue for lower-margin shoes. The favorable currency conversion tends to pay for the fees, even after considering the necessary cheaper listing price and higher shipping fees. I like to offer to "split the shipping cost" on UK eBay listings, which means I tell them in the description that I am paying half, and then I only charge them for standard shipping and ship it via priority. You'll find much less supply over here as well. The flip side of this approach is some sneakers that are popular in the US don't get much action across the pond. But it's certainly worth the try! Here is a page that explains how to list a product on the UK eBay site:

www.ebay.eu/1qCFBlP

These two free classified ad sites in the UK are like Craigslist here, and might be worth a shot now and then:

www.GumTree.co.uk

www.FreeAds.co.uk

Instead of direct Paypal invoicing, you can have your own **Shopify site** for $9 a month and make people pay there. This might convince a few timid customers to buy who wouldn't go for the Paypal invoice, as it also offers credit card payment, and it also might help you win a Paypal dispute once in a while (because you sell from an official-looking website).

Now for something a bit more ninja. Craiglist is one of the top 15 traffic sites in the US. What if you could use Craigslist to **drive traffic to your eBay listing**? No, Craigslist doesn't allow this. Like I said, you need to do it ninja-style with proxies, different email addresses, and spun ads & images. Thankfully, there is software that can help. Here's a plan for posting in 18 different Craiglist cities:

1. Get 18 gmail accounts for $5 here: **www.bit.ly/1YCmK5s**

2. Set them all on vacation response with a message explaining that you decided to sell the sneakers on eBay and provide a link to the listing.

3. Edit your image in Paint and save it 18 times into a folder each with a different name & pixel dimensions (or just use the image spinner add-on below).

4. Strip your image of EXIF data on all 18 images: **www.bit.ly/1Oo7SD8** (or just use the image spinner add-on below).

5. You need 18 US proxies. Got them this month? If not, Craiglist proxies are cheap.

6. You need this software: **www.claposter.com** (there's an add-on that will spin your image info saving you the hassle of steps 3 and 4 above)

7. Create 18 unique ads with an online article spinner like this one: **www.FreeSpinner.net** (or use the image spinner add-on available in CLAposter)

8. This Firefox gmail account manager comes in handy as well: **www.mzl.la/23Hw278**

Now you can post an ad for your sneakers in the 18 largest Craiglist cities, which you can see here: **www.bit.ly/1MCvk3F**

...using all 18 of your gmail accounts, proxies, ads, and images of course. All who inquire by email will be automatically referred to your eBay listing from your set email response. It will take you a little while to get the hang of that software, but it works, and is very affordable. You'll need a few of the add-ons like the proxy rotator and image spinner.

Of course, instead of sending the Craigslist replies to your eBay listing, you could actually try to sell by direct Paypal invoice or point them to your Shopify site. If by Paypal invoice, set the gmail accounts to all forward to one account for easier managing. And no one says you have to blast 18 cities. I've had no problems posting a slightly-spun ad (and image) to the top 5 cities all from one phone-verified Craigslist account. If using multiple emails, you'll run into the phone verification problem (which CLAposter claims to be able to get around, but I haven't had any luck with that feature personally).

Another alternative is to find Craiglist posters on **Fiverr.com**. Some of them will post an ad to 5 cities for you for five bucks. They are usually from Bangladesh where $5 USD goes a lot farther than you would imagine, and some of them are pretty good at this.

Aftermarket Flipping

We mentioned earlier that you can actually buy Yeezys at aftermarket prices and hold them expecting to make a profit months down the line. You cannot, of course, pay top dollar when so doing. You need to be a wheeler-dealer and negotiate a deal with someone who needs their working capital replenished.

Yeezys aren't the only shoe you can dabble with in the aftermarket. You can, in fact, buy and resell for a profit any high-demand product if you care to work this sideline and are diligent about it. Expect thinner margins, but this can be worth your while.

The supply will be highest on any hyped release 1-2 weeks after the drop date. This is when you can work the eBay listings looking for discouraged sellers whose listings are buried a few pages back and who aren't getting a lot of action. If they have a *Buy it Now + Best Offer* listing, hit them with a lowball offer. You never know.

Most of the time you'll be dealing with auctions when looking to buy on the aftermarket. It's pretty easy to peruse all the listings seeking the standout low prices on a particular style number. When you click the listings, most will end up being child's sizes and you'll quickly click away again.

But some will be for good adult sizes. Some of those will have 3+ days left on the auction. Forget those. But some will be ending tomorrow. Those are the ones you want to bid on and/or watch.

It should go without saying by now that you have checked the sold listings and confirmed there is daily action. You checked Flight Club and verified even higher prices. Now what you want to do is get a pair that are going for $220 for about $150 landed (including shipping) via an auction. The tactic works best if the seller's location is close to you, reducing your shipping cost.

Make sure you only deal with sellers that have established good reputation when buying on the aftermarket!

A similar method is to buy from retailers at steep **sale** prices and resell for retail. Sometimes retailers will decide to blow out a bunch of stock for something like 40% off. When this happens on a good shoe like Ultra Boosts, and you can get good sizes for something like $120 shipped and retail is $190, and the current eBay listings are all right around retail, you can go ahead and pull the trigger on a high-supply shoe you would normally never consider. These kinds of sales are usually not advertised; you find out about them by Twitter alert and need to use a special discount code. Just resell the shoes at retail or slightly below.

Aftermarket flipping isn't for everyone. But for those who are drawn to it, and have the extra capital to put to work for lower margins, it can add $500+ to your bottom line every month. And it doesn't take very long. You can do it on your laptop from the couch while watching TV. Just keep on eye on the current supply, number of sales every day, and ...be careful.

Putting it All Together

This business is a mix of organization, remaining alert, technology tricks, and fast reflexes. To what degree you can master all these elements will determine your income level. And it won't come right away. Despite the fact we've given you everything you need to succeed, we can't give you the final ingredient: experience. You'll have to get that yourself. Even if you're sharp as a tack, well-funded, and are the most motivated self-starter on planet earth, you are going to make a heck of a lot more your third month in this business than your first month. I'm not entirely sure why, but I know it with a certainty.

I want to wrap things up by breaking down the numbers and then recap everything you need to get set up. Talking about revenue is always fun, so we'll start there. With a concentrated effort, a noob in his second month ought to be able to earn the following from each avenue:

Multi-thread botting scheduled sneaker releases: **$700+**

Browser copping other scheduled sneaker releases: **$700+**

Browser copping sudden restock alerts: **$1000+**

Winning sneaker drawings: **$400+**

Supreme copping + relay resales: **$500+**

Lipkits: **$500+**

Aftermarket flipping: **$200+**

Ground game: ?

That all adds up to **$4200** in gross profits for a 2nd month newbie, and that's without any ground game. And folks, those **are** reasonably conservative numbers. At the beginning of this guide, I realize I may have insinuated that a ground game was somewhat beneath us at Hype Sniper, but I now confess that as I'm writing this I'm planning on hitting two Champs stores tomorrow that are supposed to be getting some Ultra Boosts that have easy $100 aftermarket margins. My plan is to hit them both for 2 pairs each if they have them in good sizes. I'll have to drive 15 miles to get to both stores, but *heck yeah* if I can cop $400 in profit this way I'm doing it. My eBay listings on these will be live by the end of the day. Do something like this just twice a month and ...you know the rest.

Some of you are probably surprised that I have the *manual browser copping* method making as much as your bots! All I can tell you is I actually make more from using the four Chrome windows on my server than I do with my multi-threading bots, even on scheduled releases. A lot of drops aren't botable, bots fail more often than the tweets would lead you to believe, and this figure does include using the Heated Sneaks Shopify bot – but to be honest, most of my browser copping simply utilizes Chrome auto-fill. A multi-threading bot is still well worth the investment, however.

I'm guessing the other surprising figure is sudden restocks being the single most profitable source by a noticeable margin. This is because they are, quite frankly, the easiest cops, and are more frequent. Not everyone can keep an eye on a custom-tailored Twitter feed and react quickly to opportunities that routinely have less than a half-hour's warning

– and often occur a few minutes **after** the drop, sending you scrambling. It's a decent argument for never going to the mall, because you'll certainly miss a few online restocks doing that. But there's also a lot to be said for having balance in your life. You gotta get away from the PC sometimes, right? God help us all.

Those of you with good business sense probably immediately spotted a potential obstacle to these hypothetical "second month" results: the **cost of inventory** will be in the neighborhood of $6000. Wait! Don't run away screaming. It isn't as much of a roadblock as it first appears. You'll be surprised how much of your capital can be quickly recouped through "relay sale" listings. And remember, this is your second month. If you are willing to pour everything back into the business, as most entrepreneurs should do in the beginning, your first month would have only needed around $4,000 for inventory, much of which also could have been recouped via relay listings. So if you are starting with four prepaid cards that have $500 each on them, and that's your entire bankroll, maybe it takes you a few months to work up to this level. But once you are here you can start paying yourself.

Operational Expenses

That $4200 you'll make in your hypothetical second month is gross profit, not net. Unfortunately, we're done with the fun part. Now it's time to add up our expenses. The good news is your inbound shipping costs were already included in your gross profit figures above, along with your inventory costs and seller fees. But the rest you'll have to incur. They are:

Prepaid Card Fees **$35**
Server: **$60**
Proxies: **$70**
VPN: **$10**
Outbound Shipping Fees: **$200**
Two mailing center box rentals? **$40**
Hype Sniper Membership (a no brainer) **$19**

Your total operational expenses are **$434**. Wow, those can add up fast, huh? Welcome to Business 101. That means your $4200 in gross profit only earned you about $3750. Well, that's not exactly true, seeing as all these expenses are tax-deductible. But this should open your eyes as to how important it is to keep control of your expenses. No, you can't afford high-priced Nike proxies (nor do you need them). Don't offer free shipping on your eBay listings if you can get away with charging your customer – especially on high-demand sneakers. Make sure you understand the hidden costs of this business before deciding to cop a thin-margin restock.

Don't let the operational expenses scare you away, either. The total assumes you are reselling your goods and making profits. If you don't sell anything your first month, and aren't renting any mailing center boxes, your total operational expenses **are only $194** (plus the cost of software – which makes it totally acceptable to wait and buy a bot after doing everything else for a month or two).

Also, certain small expenses like $10 monthly maintenance for a Greendot prepaid card are, in reality, no big deal in the face of this list of total expenses – especially if that card is cool with you changing your billing address to a friend's house or a mailing center box.

How to Get Started – Exactly

We've been through a lot. If you're a green-as-grass-noob, you are probably ready to start over at the beginning of this guide and read it through again. By all means, do that. And then use the following list to get set up in a logical order, step-by-step.

Step 1. Arrange four different local delivery addresses you can use, and, while you're at it, four different cell phone numbers (for Nike drawings). Get four different email accounts set up and ready for use. Begin to build a spreadsheet organizing this information.

Step 2. Withdraw $2,000 cash from your bank and go buy four different prepaid credit cards for $500 each at the drug store, supermarket, and/or convenience store. Take them home and register them online with your four different emails and addresses (maybe use your real address for a couple of them, and change it after the permanent cards arrive). Update your spreadsheet for easy reference to see which card has which address, email, and phone number associated with it.

Step 3. Rent a VPS/server. If you insist, and your home PC is a super computer, you can try running this business from a VM. Download Chrome on your server, create four different "Person" users, install the SwitchyOmega extension in each of them, and set up Auto-Fill in each of the four Chrome user-windows with your four different addresses, email addresses, phone numbers, and credit card numbers. Don't forget to change the credit card numbers after your permanent reloadable cards arrive.

Step 4. Buy proxies. This part is tricky and you need to know where to get good ones for Supreme, Nike, and the Footsites at reasonable prices. Lately the cowboys have been the way to go. Read through the recent "tweets and replies" of all the bot sellers and look for retweets of people shouting their success screenshots. Often they will mention their proxy provider in the tweet as well. Track the cowboys down this way (or if you join Hype Sniper just check our current list of recommended proxy cowboys) and ask for quotes by sending them a direct message on Twitter. If you are buying a multi-threading bot, you'll need more proxies than if you are not. If you can buy a small handful of UK proxies, those are nice to have.

Once you have the proxies, get them set up in your SwitchyOmega extensions, spreading them out in your different Chrome user windows. If you have trouble with this, and you care to join Hype Sniper, I'd be happy to help by Teamviewer.

Step 5. If you live in the US, open a free account at *Borderlinx* and *ForwardtoMe* and make note of your UK shipping addresses at these services. Maybe you won't use this for a while, but maybe you will.

Step 6. Buy software. It is recommended to get the Heated Sneaks package and one good multi-threader like BNB/AIO or EasyCop. If you are on a budget, and want to get the multi-threader after making some money web-browser copping for a month or two, I won't argue. Install the various Heated Sneaks bot extensions you plan on using in your Chrome user windows (they allow four for each bot, perfect).

Step 7. Get your Twitter account set up for the drop alerts. This means following the drop alert guys like Sole Links and Sneaker Shouts (plus a few more) and also the bot accounts, especially Heated Sneaks. Use a different web browser than you do for everything else, keep it on your Twitter home page and minimize it to your task bar where you can see at a glance if there are new tweets to read. When you notice that it suddenly has something like 14 new tweets, you can bet there's a restock alert going down.

Step 8. Have your central command center at the ready, no more than a pounce away. Your remote desktop connection to your server should be pinned to your start menu. Keep all four Chrome user windows open on your server, so all you need to do is paste in the URL you got from your Twitter feed into each window. After that it's simply a matter of choosing a good size in each window (8, 8.5, 9, 9.5, 12, 12.5, or 13) and check out using Chrome's auto-fill, as many times as you can. Many weekdays you can score 1-4 pairs of $50-150 profit shoes doing nothing but this!

Step 9. Buy some stuff on eBay if you are new. Whatever you need around the house: pet supplies, vitamins, toiletries, or whatever. You'll start building up your eBay feedback reputation this way, even if it's from being a buyer. It looks much better than not having any reputation at all, and many buyers won't check to see if it's seller reputation.

Step 10. Remember to always do market evaluation before purchasing a pair of sneakers. Fools rush in. You want to profit from the hype without being taken in by it. Check the number of listings for each size, see what the average price is, check the sold listings to see what they are actually selling for, and make note of how many daily sales are occurring. Lean towards passing if the decision is borderline!

Step 11. Create four different Nike accounts using four different IP addresses (go to Starbucks if you have to) that work at Nike.com. Add mobile numbers to the account settings and verify them via text messages so you can use all four for the drawings. Buy someone at Starbucks a coffee for letting you get a text message on their phone if you need to.

Step 12. Acquire shipping supplies: A shipping tape dispenser, postage scale, and free flat rate boxes from the post office or eBay.

Step 13. Get some experience buying and reselling. The Kylie lip kits are a great way to do this when starting out. Their drops happen several times a month. Stick with the Posie and Koko colors, and be happy making $20 each (keep in mind you can get 24 of them, 12 of each good color, using the Heated Sneaks bot on four Chrome user windows). Practice creating HTML listings, negotiating with potential customers, using the different listing types, and printing shipping labels from eBay. Have fun with these listings!

Final Thoughts

Making $50 net profit on an item that costs you $240 landed is not the same thing as making $50 net profit on a $130 landed item. The latter is **much** preferred, even if you are reselling outside of eBay. It leaves you more working capital. It protects you more from a sudden glutton of supply hitting the market. Less expensive items are generally faster to sell. Wholesale businesses care about the gross profit **percentage** on sales, not just the gross profit dollars. As an astute entrepreneur, so should you.

The hypothetical "second month" results we used as an example in the first section of this chapter works in theory. In actual practice, however, it may not, due to the ebb and flow of supply and demand in the aftermarket. We mentioned that sometimes it's best to hold an item a while before selling. Other times you end up sitting with certain products longer than it seems you should, even after building up seller reputation, even when you have a hot item. So there's a bit of a pipeline effect to this business. Once your pipeline is full, the sales will come steady on both new stock and stuff you've had a while. That's when you'll realize it's all good. Just keep filling the pipe and selling every day (but do keep a tight rein on purchasing guy). It shouldn't take more than a few months to reach this point, especially if you are well-funded for inventory when you start out.

I haven't held anything back in this guide, other than a few good Twitter sources you can easily find by using your head for something other than a hat rack. You have everything you need to succeed except experience. You don't actually need to join the Hype Sniper membership site. But wouldn't you like to come hang out with us, chat a bit, receive encouragement, and check out what products we're targeting this week? If so, read on...

Hype Sniper Membership Benefits

We'll give you a kitchen to cook from like no other for $19 per month. You'll make much more than that back the first time you cop an item we recommend, which will probably be within the next week! Join a community of experts that will put you on to the best drops to target – and, just as importantly, keep you away from the high-supply, low-margin traps.

Our member's area has all the relevant feeds piped into one place. We have a constantly-updated calendar of worthwhile drops, and all the best news sources. Early link providers' live feeds surround you. Chat with other members in real time about release rumors and strategies.

Our active forum contains a wealth of information including bot tips & reviews, retailer specifics, current resale market evaluation, which proxy cowboys are good this month, success stories, experiences with different prepaid cards, selling & shipping advice, and everything else related to this business.

We hope to see you there often, and to slap a virtual high-five on you every time you score.

If you are reading this paragraph, it means you acquired this guide without paying $79 for it (the going rate). Congratulations! You're well on your way to a successful hype sniping career. A special membership signup link has been arranged for you. Instead of $79 once + $19 monthly, you will only be charged $45 your first month + $14 monthly thereafter. Sign up here:

www.HypeSniper.com/SpecialOffer.htm

Upon completing purchase, please email us a desired username and password for accessing our kitchen, to:

Support@HypeSniper.com

Happy sniping!

Printed in Great Britain
by Amazon

34018399R00086